TOUGH-MINDED LEADERSHIP

Ten Commandments of Expective Leadership

1. I will *tell* no one. But I will *expect* much.
2. The truth is the only thing that sets you free.
3. I will diligently expect to *be* what I expect of others.
4. I will unleash, unshackle, and be proud of my enthusiasm.
5. I will search for some positive strengths in every person. I will expect each person's best.
6. I will share life, love, and laughter with my team.
7. I know that expectations are the key to all happenings.
8. I know that the best control is a clearly and mutually understood expectation.
9. I will sculpt a vision and plan boldly.
10. I will *live* my plan. I will *lead* my team!

I see myself as an instrument of human progress.

TOUGH-MINDED LEADERSHIP

JOE D. BATTEN

AMERICAN MANAGEMENT ASSOCIATION

This book is available at a special
discount when ordered in bulk quantities.
For information, contact Special Sales Department,
AMACOM, a division of American Management Association,
135 West 50th Street, New York, NY 10020.

Library of Congress Cataloging-in-Publication Data

Batten, Joe D.
   Tough-minded leadership / Joe D. Batten.
       p.   cm.
   Bibliography: p.
   Includes index.
   ISBN 0-8144-5901-3
   1. Leadership.   2. Management.   I. Title.
HD57.7.B38   1989
658.4′092—dc19   *88-48023*

Printing number

10 9 8 7 6 5 4 3 2 1

FOREWORD
by H. Ross Perot

During the early years of EDS, the company was small, had little capital, and was forced to compete head on with IBM. The EDS team offset these disadvantages by having clearly stated philosophies of how we would work together—and win.

These philosophies were carefully explained to each new person joining EDS. We wanted these philosophies to be so distinct that they would strongly attract the person to the company—or cause him *not* to join because he disagreed with our values.

As EDS grew, it became more difficult to review these philosophies with each new person. During this period, I was given a copy of Joe Batten's book, *Tough-Minded Management*. As I read it, I realized that this book was exactly what EDS needed. For many years, every person joining EDS was given a copy of *Tough-Minded Management*, with a handwritten note from me. The end result was a successful company, generally recognized as the finest in its field, and with an unmatched record for competing against and beating the giants.

Joe's new book, *Tough-Minded Leadership*, clearly, directly, and forcefully describes how to build a strong, unified team and optimize the potential of the people within the company.

I strongly recommend this book to anyone who wants to build a great organization. Success or failure will depend on the leader's ability to motivate the people, keep a results-oriented climate, build a unified team that builds the highest-quality products in its field, and looks forward to taking on all competitors in fair, open competition—and beating them soundly!

H. Ross Perot
Chairman of the Board
The Perot Group, Inc.

ACKNOWLEDGMENTS

Attempting to acknowledge even a minute portion of the "Batten-builders" who have given me so much for so many years is a formidable challenge. During the thirty-plus years of our company, BBH&S, literally hundreds of colleagues have contributed more than I can begin to acknowledge. Our consulting and training clients throughout the world provided many opportunities and privileges that have helped enrich *Tough-Minded Leadership*. Their exacting requirements help ensure that all the "theory" described in the book is researched, tested, and validated.

The original team that made up the euphemistically titled Batten & Associates in 1957 consisted of my wife, Jean, and me. Leonard Hudson joined us in 1958, and Hal Batten and Jim Swab in 1959, and we became Batten, Batten, Hudson & Swab, Inc. These men reflected the very highest standards of integrity, service, and commitment. To Jean, Hal, Jim, and Leonard goes my heartfelt gratitude. Other stars in the BBH&S firmament include Mary Roelofs, my loyal, gifted, and indispensable assistant, John Wade, Arthur Bauer, Dennis Murphy, Bob Gappa, Sharon Ward, Joyce Sullivan, Shirley Winner, Frank Russell, Don Bell, and Philip Pletcher. Other management professionals whose influence helped mold my philosophy and hence this book include such outstanding practitioners as Ross

Perot, Berkley Bedell, George Morrisey, Robert Randolph, Don Kirkpatrick, and Donald Alstadt.

I would like to thank Marty Stuckey for her talented, excellent editing.
Thanks also to AMACOM Associate Editor Barbara Horowitz, Develop-
mental Editor, Eva Weiss, and Senior Acquisitions and Planning Editor,
Adrienne Hickey.

In unique, special, and blessed ways my daughters, Gail and Wendy,
have given me more insights, discoveries, and affirmation than a dozen
fathers have the right to expect. They played catalytic roles in shaping my
values and thus our company's philosophy, which stimulated us to pioneer
in several areas, including training women for equality in the workplace
and all other dimensions—to the tune of some 3,600 public seminars in 1980
alone.

These are some of the people who helped me discover that a tough mind
and a tender heart are one. Above all, Jean's caring critiques and candor
continue to have a profound impact on all that I am. Her excellent and
devoted editorial work on this book was superb. She is in a very real sense
the co-author, but prefers to retain a low profile. After forty vibrant years
together, it is my privilege to dedicate this book to her.

INTRODUCTION:
Excellence and Beyond

When *Tough-Minded Management* was published in 1963, we all lived in a vastly different world. "Management" was thought to be an amalgam of procedures, processes, materials, and methods. People were too often perceived as necessary items of overhead. Equality in the workplace for women and minorities was scarcely mentioned. When I first used words such as *passion, vision,* and *excellence,* most American managers could not see their relationship to the world of business—but the Japanese could!

To American business leaders, the world seemed predictable; they could develop five- and ten-year projections with a good measure of confidence. Then, gradually the tempo of change accelerated. Awareness of the global community increased. And with it an uneasy feeling began to pervade boardrooms and executive offices, the feeling that something wasn't working all that well in American business. Slowly the understanding began to build that the leader was part of the problem—and a *major* part of the solution.

In the years since, much has happened in American industry—and much of it is good. The emphasis on "excellent companies" is a major achievement. But there is more we must do. Some requires a renewed focus on

ix

"old" ideas, which is why readers may find some of the key sections from *Tough-Minded Management* repeated here. In addition, we badly need to commit more resources to the growth and development of leaders as fully functioning *persons*.

My focus in this book is on the methods, procedures, processes, techniques, and many other overt manifestations of the tough-minded leader. But much more important, I address how to target and stimulate fundamental changes in the *mind* and *values* of this crucial individual. How the leader views, perceives, and responds to life as a whole, in terms of *changed behavior*, is my concern here.

Thirty years with a company that works with virtually all kinds of organizations worldwide have convinced me that when the emotional, intellectual, and spiritual components—the attitudes—are right, the actions are right.

In a world where exponential adaptive change is called for, where what is new today is obsolete tomorrow, we must place an absolute premium on training *minds* above all. If the minds of leaders are tough, strong, open, resilient, and hungry for positive innovation, true greatness lies ahead. Tough-mindedness takes much more than mental agility. Tenacity, stamina, clarity, discipline, and depth—these are key requisites for the mentally tough executive of tomorrow.

Recently, I was interviewed by a very impressive MBA candidate. Her questions were pertinent and penetrating, and did an excellent job of zeroing in on the key concepts. Because it seems to encapsulate most of what I consider the truly important points of this book, I believe that interview makes a fine introduction to the book as a whole.

Q.: Today, we see a greater emphasis on management style and philosophy. What, in your opinion, is the newest development?

A.: Leadership by expectation. It's a new style of leadership, one that requires fundamental changes at a very deep level in management attitudes. Basically, it means this: *we become what we expect*. There is a direct link between what we expect from ourselves and our team members, and what we and they actually achieve in terms of results that contribute directly to the company's profits.

Q.: How does leadership by expectation differ from traditional management concepts now used by American industry?

A.: The majority of managers today still manage by directive: they tell, push, drive. They pigeonhole people into boxes on an organization chart. Leadership by expectation expects the best from each person and gives them goals they can reach if they stretch. Then it holds them accountable for results, rewarding performance that contributes to corporate goals. At the same time, leaders set the example by their own attitudes. They give their people a model to follow. There is no separation between what they say and what they do.

Q.: Where does leadership by expectation differ from management by objectives, or MBO?

A.: It goes beyond MBO. To get the best results, you must do more than merely establish goals and objectives. You have to get your people involved first so they will make a *commitment* to those goals.

Q.: What does it take to get this kind of result?

A.: Leaders must be willing to take the time to sit down and develop a real understanding of the drives and ambitions of each team member and to encourage that potential in each one. Then they will get the synergistic effect they need to increase the productivity of the team.

Q.: How do a leader's expectations create a climate for results?

A.: When the majority of your people realize that the best way to achieve their own personal goals is to perform in such a way that they contribute to company profits, then and only then will you have a motivational climate for results. Control, you see, does not come from the outside. It is the self-control that comes from enlightened, involved, and committed people working together as a team. The difference between ordinary light and a potent laser beam is the degree of focus and intensity.

Q.: What does this require of a leader?

A.: It requires a certain toughness. Expectations are far stronger than directives, and they achieve much greater results. Yet for many managers, it is easier to give orders than develop people. It takes a tough-minded leader to lead by expectations. It requires courage to take risks, to change attitudes, to stick your neck out and walk in front of the flock.

Q.: How does this management philosophy work in today's high-technology world?

A.: Well, look at IBM, one of the most profitable companies in the world. They use leadership by expectation, building on strengths rather than focusing on people's weaknesses. They have discovered the tough-minded principle that *our strengths are our tools!* In *A Business and Its Beliefs: The Ideas That Helped Build IBM*, Thomas Watson, Jr., says that IBM owes its success to the belief that "the basic philosophy, spirit, and drive of an organization have far more to do with its relative achievements than do technological or economic resources, organizational structure, innovation and timing. Our most important belief," he adds, "is our respect for the individual. This is a simple concept but in IBM it occupies a major portion of management time. We devote more effort to it than anything else."[1] IBM knows that true leadership is of, by, about, and for people.

1. (Ann Arbor, Mich.: UMI).

Q.: Why is it important to build on a person's strengths?

A.: This is the heart of leading by expectation, and it is crucial. All too often we tend to judge people, pointing out all the things they do wrong. We should, in fact, evaluate them by searching for their strong points and helping them develop these further. This does not mean that we ignore their areas of weakness; we acknowledge them, but we do not focus all our attention on them.

Q.: How does a leader build on strengths?

A.: First, identify each person's strengths, both existing and potential. Where can you use them to help you achieve departmental goals? Then, when you are setting performance standards, challenge your people to meet stretching goals based on these strengths. *Reinforce* these strengths—that's what positive reinforcement is all about. And expect excellence from them. Hold them accountable for results and reward them for the results they achieve. Continuous feedback and compensation based on results will foster a climate where each person uses self-control to improve performance. Also, be sure to give earned praise unstintingly; there is nothing more truly motivational.

Q.: How can a leader increase performance levels?

A.: Performance is based on people. Performance will improve only when people improve. Well-written performance standards are certainly expectations, but they must be specific. They must define the results required, and in terms that can be measured. And they must progressively provide more "stretching" goals to give people something to reach for. They provide a valid basis for truly positive reinforcement.

Q.: How do leaders' attitudes affect the performance of their people?

A.: As leaders we have a choice. We can mold and compress a person to fit a job that has been carefully tied into other jobs. Or we can encourage people to expand their capabilities and become part of a dynamically growing organization. We can drive, or we can lead. We can compress, repress, and depress by pushing—or we can stretch, exemplify, and lead.

Q.: In other words, you expect a great deal not only from your team but from yourself as well?

A.: That's right. True leaders know that real authority rests not in their position in the management hierarchy. It rests in the person, by the very example set daily. I challenge managers today to manage as though they held no rank, as though they had to depend on the quality of their ideas and the example they set to have people follow them. If you, as leader, held no title, would your people still follow you? What you are speaks more loudly than what you say.

Q.: We have to think big, then? We have to offer people a chance to feel a part of something greater?

A.: Absolutely. All too often, we underestimate people. Masters of motivation, however, know that the single most important factor in leadership is to inspire commitment to a cause greater than self. The so-called leader who pushes, drives, and compresses is out of date and thoroughly counter-productive. The real leader encourages people to grow, innovate, and thrive. Pushers and drivers are a dime a dozen. Business needs real leaders as never before.

CONTENTS

TOUGH-MINDED LEADERSHIP

CHAPTER 1

THE NEXT DECADE BECKONS

The dogmas of the quiet past are inadequate for the stormy present and future. As our circumstances are new, we must think anew, and act anew.

ABRAHAM LINCOLN

The decade of the 1980s has witnessed a volatile series of changes in the way leadership is viewed in America.

Increasingly, it is moving beyond the level of craft to the level of profession. What we need now is a commitment to further elevate it to the level of *art*. Now, as never before, we need a breed of leaders committed to a new, tough-minded paradigm: the *art* of leadership. Leadership must be our *first* national priority.

A number of books have appeared in recent years in which the current practices of successful executives are chronicled. In this book I propose to focus on leaders as individuals, and to share suggestions, insights, and tools to guide and stimulate those who aspire to exemplify the word *excellence*.

1

Successful, productive organizations are made possible only by successful, productive individuals working together, with confidence, commitment, synergy, and joy.

As we look searchingly ahead, the need for certain transitions becomes clear. There are nine crucial changes that must occur if American business is to move again into the vanguard of world commerce. I present them here as a kind of "preview"; they are key themes in this text, and I'll be talking about them throughout the book.

From	*To*
1. Competing with other nations	Competing with our own possibilities
2. Mere number crunching	Intuitive sensing, feeling, sculpting
3. Rigid, static practices	Mental agility and suppleness
4. Directiveness	Expectiveness
5. Passive protectionism	Passionate stretching
6. High tech / high touch	High touch / high tech
7. Glittering generalities	Tough-minded action steps
8. Mental flabbiness	Mental toughness
9. Frozen cultures	Organic cultures

THE DIFFERENCE BETWEEN A LEADER AND A MANAGER

Managers abound but leaders are still at a premium. Managers manage inventories, supplies, and data. They are numbers crunchers. Leaders catalyze, stretch, and enhance people. They provide transcendent goals, creating a motive-ational climate.

Managers *push* and direct. Leaders pull and expect. Leaders are exhilarated by identifying and enhancing their people's strengths.

Despite the many books on management published in recent years, the MBA factories continue to turn out graduates woefully deficient in leadership insights, skills, and hands-on tools. Taking refuge behind reams of data is still appallingly common, but it is no substitute for true leadership.

The very nature of management must be perceived in a new way. In practical reality, management is an ever-changing, ever-dynamic system of interacting minds. In the future—and the future is almost here—managing minds and spirits will be the name of the game.

THE CUSTOMER IS NUMBER-ONE PRIORITY

The counterpuncher, the reactor, is never world class, whether in sports, politics, or business. Leaders are committed *above all* to customer sensitivity, skillfully and continuously determining and assessing the wants, needs, and possibilities of their current and potential customers. They listen regularly and intently. They may even be somewhat manic about it. By word, precept, and example they will constantly send messages to their teams that the customer is the alpha and omega of their business, the number-one priority at all times.

This must go far beyond empty rhetoric and breast beating. Uttering pious pronouncements about being "dedicated to service" and "committed to excellence" is not enough. In fact, such claims are becoming *counter*productive in many organizations where action plans are conspicuous by their absence. Rhetoric without demonstrable followthrough creates disillusionment in customers and employees alike.

Leaders must ensure that all segments of the organization are consistently, relentlessly responsive to the finest and most sensitive information from customers. All bulletin boards, meeting agenda, memoranda, press releases must reflect this focus. Performance-appraisal criteria must be built in so that all rewards are related squarely to this emphasis. Evaluation systems and procedures must be developed around the notion that the relative importance of each position will be tied directly to impact on customers. The highest salary grades will be for those jobs that have the most powerful impact on the customer.

Robert Lookabaugh, chairman of Eye Max, Inc., a nationwide consortium of optometrists, is pioneering methods that use computer technology to assess customer needs and possibilities so thoroughly at point of sale that this information becomes virtually the sole basis for strategy, tactics, and decisions. One of the great new leaders, he is illustrating how the traditional concept of competition is becoming secondary, or even tertiary. The customer is *first*. The excellent organization of tomorrow can base all its competitive strategy on this approach. The traditional competition then has to *react* and counterpunch, tactics that usually result in "also-ran" performance and diminished profits.

Lookabaugh says, "Our incredible strength is that our clients are the on-site connection to the essence of the business. They are the foundation or anchor. We can focus clearly on goals that do not change; satisfying the customer remains constant."

Truly excellent companies compete with themselves—with their own self-generated objectives and possibilities.

A LEADER'S TOOLBOX

Tomorrow's leaders will be, above all, mentally tooled for the decades ahead. Pushed and driven organizations will certainly lose out to those that are led and stretched. We must release old habits and consign them to the past. The cold, hard, rigid driver is out. The leading, stretching, expective, intuitive leader plugged into productive, future-oriented attitudes (which I call positive G forces, and which I'll define further later on) is in. The orderly, antiseptic climate is out. The yeasty, fermentive, and volatile climate is in.

In the vernacular of sheepherding, the opposite of the leader, who walks in front of the flock, is the all-too-common driver, who walks behind the flock. Such a "leader" is no leader at all; rather, he or she is a pusher who compresses, represses, and depresses the people in the flock. Such an obsolete manager tends to use phrases such as *value driven, customer driven, market driven*. These are regressive forces binding us to the past.

The true leader believes in, teaches, and exemplifies the concept of "-led"—people *led*, value *led*, data *led*, customer *led*. At a premium, always, is the confidence, the strengths orientation needed to *pro*act, to walk in *front* of the flock. These are the forces pulling the team into the future.

Change can frighten, depress, and paralyze, or it can challenge, stretch, and enrich. Since we can't avoid it, our only reasonable option is to anticipate it and prepare for it. The new leader will cultivate flexibility, mental suppleness, and resilience. Rigid thinking and defensive action have no place in the toolbox of the new leader. Peak performers—winners—are motivated by passionate commitment to a transcendent vision, dream, or mission.

Winners and losers alike carry a toolbox on their shoulders. Increasingly, tough-minded, visioneering executives will fully comprehend that in the Age of the Mind, the tools we use have no chemical composition. Ideas are our tools. Ideas and thoughts are the catalyst of all innovation, all action, all knowledge, all information, all service, all bottom-line achievements. The race for inner space is truly the number-one priority of the tough-minded leader of the future.

Thus our toolboxes can contain blunt implements (directives) that bruise and abrade, or exquisite precision instruments (expectives) that build and enrich. Careful defense strategies will not be sufficient for the volatile world that lies ahead. Calculated openness and vulnerability are key parts of the new tough-minded wave. Responsiveness to the customer and the willingness to risk and dare will be the keys to all unusual success stories.

PEOPLE FIRST, TECHNOLOGY SECOND

Many high-tech companies aspire to be as successful as IBM, but few of them have IBM's clear vision about the relative value of people and technology. High technology is truly a marvelous tool, but it is only a tool.

In 1969, in a seminar for IBM people in Carmel, California, I read from a pithy book called *A Business and Its Beliefs*, written by Thomas Watson, Jr., former CEO of IBM. In the book, Watson flatly states that IBM is *not* a technical company but a *people* company. More time, money, and total resources are invested in human resources than anything else. As a result, he says, IBM's technology and profitability were "satisfactory"—surely the understatement of the decade.

Since that 1969 seminar, a number of the participants have become leaders of Silicon Valley companies. Sadly, most of them have focused on technology first and people second. Their bottom lines and eventual mergers have reflected that myopia. In seeking to emulate IBM's success, they missed the crucial point completely.

I suggest a number of specific steps to ensure people primacy at all times:

1. Review all key items of "yeast" in your corporate culture, starting with your policy and procedure manual. Does every statement and proviso enhance "people" possibilities?
2. Do your performance-appraisal and job-evaluation procedures illustrate "people primacy"?
3. Do programs, practices, and facilities reflect this emphasis?
4. Do all your procedures reflect an emphasis on human strengths rather than weaknesses?
5. Are all performance standards worded expectively rather than directively?
6. Are you an expector or director? Directors are a dime a dozen. Expectors are at a premium and in high demand.

John Naisbitt's popular term *high tech/high touch* seems to at least suggest that technology is first and people are secondary. It is important to reverse this emphasis. The tough-minded leader *always* gives high touch primacy over high tech. In short, people first—technology second.

For mentally flabby or hard-minded managers who currently believe technology is primary and people secondary, the future will increasingly provide frustration, difficulty, failure, and heartbreak. Tough-minded visioneers are committed to reversing these priorities. They will insist that while new technology can yield marvelous breakthroughs, it must be viewed as subordinate to people, as servant rather than master.

Interestingly, high technology will achieve its greatest gains when it is deployed within the understanding that all technology, and the virtual miracles in knowledge and information it can provide, are of, by, about, and for people.

PERFORMANCE IS THE ALPHA AND OMEGA

The tough-minded leader will clearly perceive that human effort can and must be focused like a laser beam. There is real dignity in knowing that you are expected to do your best and that your best is the sum of your current and potential strengths at a given point. Just as particles of light in the usual diffused form have nothing like the practical value of a laser beam, which is fused, focused, centered, intensified light, a person very much needs this same integration and focus.

Harold Geneen, former chairman of AT&T, supplies excellent focus:

Performance is what it's all about—there is no other. Performance alone is the best measure of confidence, competence, and courage. Only performance gives you the freedom to grow as yourself.[1]

PERFORMANCE, MARRIOTT STYLE

J. Willard Marriott, chairman of the board of the enormously successful hotel chain, was recently asked: "How do you manage to be fair and nice with people and yet demand excellence from them?"

"Well, it's tough-minded management, which basically says that you treat people right and fair and decent, and in return they give their all for you."

Executive Excellence, April, 1986, p. 5.

Arthur Bauer is truly an exemplar of the great new leader. He is founder, president, and CEO of American Media, Inc., which creates training and educational media for business and distributes its products worldwide. Bauer described his philosophy in a personal letter to me:

I believe that the secrets of life (and motivation) can be summed up in one word—growth. That's the secret. That's why we're all here, to help something grow. Managers must take the responsibility to help ourselves, our families, our companies, our departments, our employees, and even our grass to grow.

There is really only one reason why each and every team member is working in a company and organization, and that is to meet their own goals and objectives, which are directly related to growth for themselves and their application of helping something else grow, be it a client, a customer, their department, or another team member. And I guess it all boils down to that famous four-letter word, love. If every goal and action is motivated and initiated from love, we simply can't go wrong.[2]

---

1. Geneen with Alvin Moscow, *Managing* (New York: Doubleday, 1984).
2. Used with permission of Arthur Bauer.

Perhaps the finest thing you can give another person is the gift of an excellent and stretching expectation; based on a never-ending search for his or her existing and potential strengths. Caring enough to *expect* the very best from people empowers their dreams and dignity.

RESILIENT MINDS AND OPEN HEARTS

What some have characterized as "flabby management" is indeed widely practiced in this country. The answer to flabbiness, however, is *not* hardness or knee-jerk reactions using compressive force. Using rank as the first expedient has no place in the toolbox of the tough-minded leader.

We must place a premium on developing the kind of sensing and intuitive skills that can flow only from a mind that is tough, resilient, open, and questing, and from a heart that truly loves all customers and all members of the team. *Resilience* is the central quality from which all other growth will flow!

In a paper titled "Toward a Theory of Creativity," the psychologist Carl Rogers says:

The creative (intuitive) person is open to his own experiences. It means a lack of rigidity and the permeability of boundaries in concepts, beliefs, perceptions and hypotheses. It means the ability to receive much conflicting ambiguity where ambiguity exists. It means the ability to receive much conflicting information without forcing closure on the situation.

Note my emphasis on certain words in this quotation.

Carl Jung, the great contemporary of Freud, described a key component of the tough mind when he said of intuitive responses: "It is a function that explores the unknown, senses possibilities and implications which may not be readily apparent."

ARE YOU A LEADER?

Leaders of the future should ask themselves these questions:

☐ *Am I just* listening *to my people or do I really* hear? Listening helps develop dialogue (two or more people engaged in monologues). Really *hearing* requires shared meaning and shared understanding—which is my definition of real communication.
☐ *What is primary here, people or technology?*
☐ *How effectively could I lead if I had no organizational authority?* Would they follow me and do what I ask if I had to depend on the quality of my ideas expressed through my example?

☐ *Am I really committed to discovering the liberating and synergistic power of love?* When Vince Lombardi was asked the secret of the Green Bay Packers' success, he replied, "These guys *love* each other!"

☐ *Do I fully understand the enormous difference between* hard-*mindedness and* tough-*mindedness?*

The new leaders will be transformers, changers. The new leaders will dare to dream—and then put muscle into those dreams.

In the words of Thomas R. Horton:

Successful chief executives seek balanced advice but still need a perceptual objectivity to make a balanced decision. Possessing the will to decide, they are tough-minded, willing to live with their decisions, regardless of the result. While they insist on tough-mindedness in their people, they also hold themselves fully accountable for the consequences of their own decisions, right or wrong. In short, they exercise decisiveness informed by balanced judgment.[3]

---

3. *"What Works for Me": Sixteen CEOs Talk About Their Careers and Commitments* (New York: Random House, 1986).

CHAPTER 2

THE ANATOMY OF LEADERSHIP

The leader who expects his people to perform their best will achieve the greatest results.

Truly excellent companies, such as IBM, Marriott, and Electronic Data Systems, have known for years that corporate values and beliefs should be stretching, evocative, and transcendent. They pull, rather than push. They fuse and focus energy and commitment. They vitalize and energize. They unhitch from the negative forces of the past and plug into the positive forces of the future.

The times cry out for quantum leaps in:

☐ Renewal   ☐ Communication
☐ Warmth   ☐ Sharing
☐ Caring   ☐ Loving
☐ Emotional vulnerability   ☐ Leading

☐ Tough and tenacious will   ☐ Stretching
☐ Motivation   ☐ Expecting the best, and posi-
☐ Intuitive thinking   tively reinforcing it

The wonderful thing is that at last, after much research and observation, we are able to perceive that such values and beliefs in action are not just nice-sounding humanistic words, but productivity imperatives. It is time for us to mobilize this arsenal of tough-minded values more effectively and forge them into systems for new levels of productivity and innovation. If we do that, we can again become leaders of the world in productivity and profit!

STRONG LEADERSHIP ENHANCES PRODUCTIVITY

There is an abundance of literature available on the basic elements of the management process—how to plan, organize, execute, coordinate, and control. By and large, however, American managers have seemed to shy away from the very elements that the Japanese have used with such success in their ascendancy to world leadership in productivity.

Students of Japanese productivity methods have identified four emphases at the very heart of their approach:

1. Spiritual values—an integral part of organization, philosophy, policies, methods, and practices
2. Self-confidence—a basic asset that fuels innovation, energy, and creativity
3. Fitness—physical, mental, and spiritual, and the programs needed to achieve it
4. Happiness—stimulated by fitness, confidence, involvement, and group activities

It would be tragic indeed if the United States backs away from the full deployment of these elements just when pragmatic experience is revealing that they are the "secret" of high productivity and morale. The knowledge is available. At a premium in this country have been the tenacity, wisdom, and courage necessary to apply this knowledge. Another necessary focus, as I'll say again and again, is that excellent leadership is not value *driven* but rather value *led*.

Do you *care* enough about your people to search out their strengths, their best possibilities—and expect their best? If you do, there are some specific things you can do to foster a climate of heightened productivity. We'll call them

Eight Steps to Increasing Team Productivity

1. Identify the strengths that all team members show in work situations. Ask them to list their own. Tie strengths directly to job contributions.
2. Classify these strengths in three categories: decision making or evaluation, problem solving or analysis, and communications or "people" skills. Rate proficiency in each area. Where is more training needed?
3. Develop these strengths through challenging assignments that stretch, combined with outside courses.
4. Assign strengths where they will benefit the company the most. Do not be boxed in by traditional roles. First look at your goals, then decide who can best help you meet them. Move decisively to establish a computerized strengths bank (more about this later in the book).
5. Set high expectations through performance objectives, mutually agreed to, and hold each person accountable for results. Blend personal goals with corporate goals to achieve a synergistic effect.
6. Measure strengths and monitor progress made toward goals. Recognize improvement, no matter how small.
7. Use feedback and self-control by each person to keep performance levels high. Compensate people directly for the results they produce.
8. Give complete primacy to strong and focused *minds*.

FROM GLITTERING GENERALITIES
TO TOUGH-MINDED SPECIFICS

How realistic is all this? Is it possible to practice a style of leadership based on the belief that a tough mind and a tender heart are one? Yes! The compleat leader of the future will possess a synergistic blend of both.

Do your people know exactly what you expect of them? Have you clearly defined policies and performance standards? Do your performance appraisals help them improve through constructive criticism, identification of strengths, and areas for further training? Start with a rigorous review of all policies and procedures, to ensure that your organization is value *led* rather than value *driven*. Provide training programs and individual mentoring to make sure everyone in the organization understands and can effectively use the tools of leadership. Be sure everyone knows why stereotyped "management" must become part of the past.

Eleven Practical Building Blocks

Here are eleven steps that have been used in many vanguard companies led by tough-minded visioneers:

1. Research, develop, and clearly communicate the company's vision, philosophy, mission, goals, and objectives. People's aspirations are focused on these transcendent motives and they move forward in concert. Involvement of the team is crucial, or commitment will be lacking. People support what they help create!
2. Use computers to create a "strengths bank" containing the key strengths of all team members. Use the "logical deployment of strengths" principle as the basis for all new personnel assignments.
3. Work with each person to develop stretching performance standards based on results. Such targeted results are components of the organization's philosophy, mission, goals, key results areas, and action plans.
4. Establish accountability for results in all key jobs and require lean, clear progress reports.
5. Regularly evaluate the worth of every department, position, and person in the organization in terms of measurable contribution to agreed-upon results. Relate all compensation and perquisites directly to performance.
6. Establish the philosophy that excellent management is the development and optimal leadership of *people*, not the direction of *things*. Assign a high priority to whole-person development.
7. Make sure all key personnel receive in-depth training in cutting-edge techniques of empowering people so that they exhibit optimal performance.
8. Provide for motivation components that include:
   a. Fulfilling basic needs for security, oppportunity, recognition, belonging, and, above all, significance
   b. Empowering optimal performance, expecting the best
   c. Positive, open listening and hearing
   d. Building on strengths
9. Develop the realization that stretching, innovation-fed *work* is a pleasant and rewarding part of life.
10. Establish and exemplify the belief that integrity is the most important ingredient in all human activity. Popularize the phrase "leadership by integrity" within your organization.
11. Establish a companywide program of physical, mental, and spiritual fitness.

The Marriott Way

One of the most successful companies in America is the Marriott Corporation, founded by J. Willard Marriott, Sr. When Bill Jr. became executive vice-president, Bill Sr. passed on these fifteen tough-minded guideposts:

1. Keep physically fit, mentally and spiritually strong.
2. Guard your habits; bad ones will destroy you.
3. Pray about every difficult problem.
4. Study and follow professional management principles. Apply them logically to your organization.
5. People are number one—their growth, loyalty, interest, team spirit. Develop managers in every area. This is your prime responsibility.
6. Decisions: Men grow making decisions and assuming responsibility for them.
   a. Make crystal clear what decision each manager is responsible for and what decisions you reserve for yourself.
   b. Have all facts and counsel necessary—then decide and stick to it.
7. Criticism: Don't criticize people, but make a fair appraisal of their qualifications with their supervisor only (or someone assigned to do this). Remember, anything you say about someone may (and usually does) get back to them. There are few secrets.
8. See the good in people and try to develop those qualities.
9. Inefficiency: If it cannot be overcome and an employee is obviously incapable of the job, find a job he can do or terminate *now*. Don't wait.
10. Manage your time.
    a. Keep conversations short and to the point.
    b. Make every minute on the job count.
    c. Work fewer hours; some of us waste half our time.
11. Delegate and hold accountable for results.
12. Details:
    a. Let your staff take care of them.
    b. Save your energy for planning, thinking, working with department heads, promoting new ideas.
    c. Don't do anything someone else can do for you.
13. Ideas and competition:
    a. Ideas keep the business alive.
    b. Know what your competitors are doing and planning.
    c. Encourage all management to think about better ways and give suggestions on anything that will improve business.
    d. Spend time and money on research and development.
14. Don't try to do an employee's job for him; counsel and suggest.
15. Think objectively and keep a sense of humor. Make the business fun for you and others.[1]

1. *Executive Excellence* (April 1986). Used by permission of J. W. Marriott, Jr.

THE CORE OF TOUGH-MINDED LEADERSHIP

So, having looked at both general philosophy and specific action steps, we can summarize some basic beliefs of the tough-minded leader:

☐ Pervasive flexibility in all elements of the culture.
☐ Performance is all that matters.
☐ Optimal service through optimum development of *people*.
☐ Expectations that stretch rather than directives that compress.
☐ Intuitive, sensing management.
☐ Clear, no-nonsense accountability for results.
☐ Build on strengths; don't dwell on weaknesses.
☐ Vision and strategy fueled by a tough, growing mind.
☐ Commitment to transcendent and growing, changing dreams.
☐ Ethical behavior, in the deepest sense.
☐ Hard and dedicated *work*.

The same central ideas are displayed pictorially in Figure 2.1.

The cybernetic circle of becoming illustrates the macro beliefs, values, and procedural fundamentals that will undergird all the ideas in this book. This circle provides the human interaction components needed to fuel the entire tough-minded leadership paradigm. All staffing, planning, coordination, execution, control, and cultural growth are to be nurtured by these elements. The meaning of the term *cybernetic* is explained in the Glossary.

U.S. LEADERS SPEAK OUT

It is perhaps fitting to close this chapter with some comments from those who practice the principles of tough-minded leadership. We might think of the quotes that follow as the "distilled wisdom" of some of America's best business minds.

> *Getting the order is the easiest step; after-sales*
> *service is what counts. Above all, we seek a*
> *reputation for doing the little things well.*[2]
> BUCK RODGERS, FORMER SALES VICE-PRESIDENT, IBM

> *In the best institutions, promises are kept no matter*
> *what the cost in agony and overtime.*[3]
> DAVID OGILVY, CHAIRMAN, OGILVY & MATHER

2. *Getting the Best Out of Yourself and Others* (New York: Harper & Row, 1987).
3. *Ogilvy on Advertising* (New York: Vintage Trade Books, 1985).

Figure 2.1. The cybernetic circle of becoming.

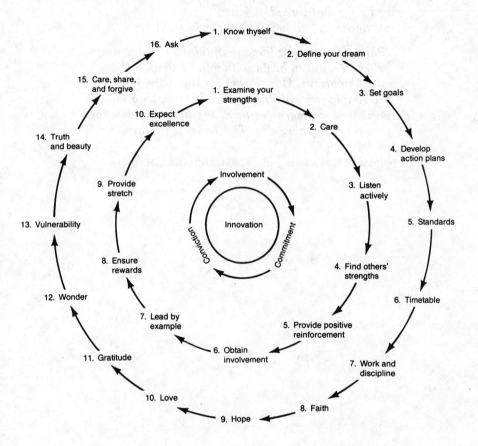

You've got to be willing to fail.[4]
JAMES E. BURKE, CHAIRMAN, JOHNSON & JOHNSON

The key ingredient is productivity through people,
pure and simple.[5]
RENÉ MCPHERSON, CEO, DANA CORPORATION

I want all our people to believe they are working in
the best organization in the world. Kill grimness

4. Thomas R. Horton, *"What Works for Me": Sixteen CEOs Talk About Their Careers and Commitments* (New York: Random House, 1986).
5. Thomas Peters and Nancy Austin, *A Passion for Excellence* (New York: Random House, 1985).

with laughter. Encourage exuberance. Get rid of
bad dogs that spread gloom.[6]
DAVID OGILVY, CHAIRMAN, OGILVY & MATHER

IBM's philosophy is largely contained in three simple
beliefs. I want to begin with what I think is the
most important. Our respect for the individual. *This*
is a simple concept, but in IBM it occupies a major
portion of management time. We devote more effort
to it than anything else. This belief was bone-deep
in my father.[7]
THOMAS J. WATSON, JR., FORMER CHAIRMAN, IBM

6. *Ogilvy on Advertising* (New York: Vintage Trade Books, 1985).
7. *A Business and Its Beliefs: The Ideas That Helped Build IBM* (Ann Arbor, Mich.: UMI).

CHAPTER

HIGH PERFORMANCE:
THE POSSIBLE DREAM

One of the most consistent characteristics among
high-performance people is the ability to take a hit
in stride and bounce back.

What's the hottest thing in management today? Leadership! I truly
believe that this new emphasis is much more than a passing fad. It is finally
being perceived by large and small organizations alike that a company's
profit and future are only as strong as its corporate culture. And an excellent
corporate culture can be envisioned and built only by excellent leaders.

A "culture" is literally "the things we believe in and the way we do
them here." The culture is founded on a carefully researched, designed,
and communicated philosophy—a statement of basic beliefs and values, a
grand design, a transcendent set of goals, a vision, a dream . . . call it what
you will.

Figure 3.1. The "P" pyramid.

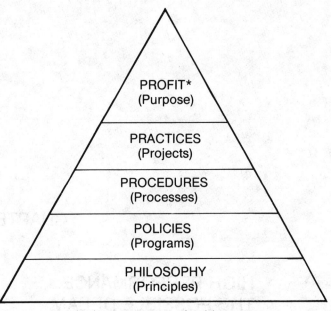

*And other measures of achievement

Take a look at the "P" pyramid (Figure 3.1). The philosophy is the broad bottom foundation. Rising out of those carefully defined principles and beliefs are the following Ps in order: policies, programs, procedures, processes, projects, and practices for the purpose of profit.

As we prepare to take dead aim on performance as the central motor of any organization, please study the "P" pyramid. It has been used as the centerpiece for many Japanese training programs. Performance, however, is the major P that all the other Ps are about.

BUILD CORPORATE CULTURES
FROM YOUR "P" PYRAMID

All excellent leaders or executives (and they should be the same people) operate according to a grand design, although some can articulate it better than others. The point is that the grand design should be researched, clearly thought out, put in writing, and communicated so pervasively and meaningfully throughout the organization that it provides the fuel for involvement, commitment, and dedication by each and every person. After all, the foundation determines just how tall a building can be. Similarly, the grand design, the basic philosophy, determines the organization's scope and purpose, the heights of service and profitability to which it may eventually rise.

Here is an example of a tough-minded mission statement:

We will provide the best customer service in the world. All decisions, all rewards, and all accountability will be conditioned by that commitment.

A superlative philosophy/mission statement is exemplified in the leadership pledge of the Marriott Corporation, as follows:

TO: *Myself*
SUBJECT: *A Pledge for (year): A Rededication to Excellence in Leadership*

I promise the members of my team:

1. *To set the right example for them by my own actions in all things.*
2. *To be consistent in my temperament so that they know how to "read" me and what to expect from me.*
3. *To be fair, impartial, and consistent in matters relating to work rules, discipline, and rewards.*
4. *To show a sincere, personal interest in them as individuals without becoming overly "familiar."*
5. *To seek their counsel on matters that affect their jobs and to be guided as much as possible by their judgment.*
6. *To allow them as much individuality as possible in the way their jobs are performed, as long as the quality of the end result is not compromised.*
7. *To make sure they always know in advance what I expect from them in the way of conduct and performance on the job.*
8. *To be appreciative of their efforts and generous in praise of their accomplishments.*
9. *To use every opportunity to teach them how to do their jobs better and how to help themselves advance in skill level and responsibility.*
10. *To show them that I can "do" as well as "manage" by pitching in to work beside them when my help is needed.*

*Signed*_____

And if all is not well with the organization, and cultural change is needed, it is up to the leader to orchestrate that change. In "The Worth

Ethic vs. the Work Ethic" (*Executive Excellence*, February 1988), management consultant Larry Senn says,

> *Leaders must cast different shadows if the culture is to change. Exec-*
> *utives must give more time and attention to the new values if the cul-*
> *ture is to change.*

It is a particular joy—and it is all too rare—to walk into an organization and hear enlightened answers to questions like these:

- [ ] Why does the company do what it does?
- [ ] What does it really believe in?
- [ ] What is the fundamental purpose of your job?
- [ ] Do you know the what, where, when, who, how, and why of your job?
- [ ] What are the organization's strengths?
- [ ] What are *your* strengths?
- [ ] Do you know what *excellence* really means?
- [ ] Do you really feel a significant part of things here?
- [ ] Are people doing things *for* each other or *to* each other?
- [ ] Is renewal going on at all levels in the organization?

Excellent organizations strive for better understanding and development of their people. The excellent organization of today and tomorrow
will be characterized by the following qualities, traits, and practices:

- [ ] Purpose and direction
- [ ] Clear, lean, and clean Ps
- [ ] Upbeat and positive attitudes
- [ ] Compensation related to actual performance
- [ ] Commitment to superior service in all dimensions and at all levels
- [ ] Zest for change
- [ ] Tomorrow-mindedness
- [ ] Feelings of involvement
- [ ] Commitment to growth and innovation
- [ ] Commitment to renewal

For those who aspire to excellence as leaders, there has never been a
more exciting time to be alive on this planet.

HOW TO BE TOUGH: A CASE STUDY

Tough-minded leaders build cultures in which all considerations of race,
sex, age, education, seniority, formal education, and all the rest are *sec-*
ondary to actual performance. Perhaps I can best illustrate this by telling
you about a young woman I know.

The Story of Ann

In about an hour the seminar on tough-minded management would be getting underway. I had arrived early to be sure that all arrangements and facilities were in good order. Hearing a sound, I turned around from the easel I was adjusting and saw a young woman walking toward me with almost military precision.

"I've been looking forward to today for quite a while," she said intensely. "Can you assure me I'll really be a tough-minded manager after this seminar?" She seemed tense and determined, wore severely tailored clothes, and looked at me almost defiantly.

I asked her what she thought a tough-minded manager was and received an all too familiar (and hopelessly outdated) summing up. In her view, a tough-minded manager is:

- ☐ *Aggressive*
- ☐ *A go-getter*
- ☐ *Assertive (the stereotyped, self-serving definition)*
- ☐ *Able to take care of yourself*
- ☐ *A winner at corporate infighting*
- ☐ *Someone who believes in "power" dressing, "power" breakfasts, and other superficial trappings of confidence*
- ☐ *Unflappable and highly controlled*
- ☐ *A pusher*
- ☐ *A driver*
- ☐ *A taker*

As we talked it became clear that she saw herself as a person who had to react and respond to a world created and dominated by men. I assured her that the path she had described was almost certain to bring about a collision with failure and asked her to be prepared for a day of discussion, involvement, emotional vulnerability, and openness.

When everyone had arrived, we began our day. The seminar focused on key transitions from the status quo to the demanding but immensely rewarding requirements of tough-mindedness in the workplace. We developed action steps for changing all the items in the left-hand column below to those on the right.

Making the Tough-Minded Transition

From	*To*
Directiveness	*Expectiveness*
Compromising expectations	*Clear, stretching expectations*
Defensiveness	*Open, warm, thoughtful candor*

From	To
Activity documents and reports	*Performance progress reports*
Hunch and guess	*Disciplined, researched decisions*
Inconsistency and emotionalism	*Consistency and focus*
Conformity or rebellion	*Individuality and competition with self*
Competing with others (the amateur)	*Competing with self (the pro)*
Complexity	*Simplicity*
Procrastination	*Confrontation*
Euphemism	*Specificity*
Dialogue (two or more people engaged in monologues)	*Communication (shared meaning, shared understanding)*
Crises and fire fighting	*"Early warning systems"*
Office politics and defensiveness	*Team synergy and openness*
Blurred, expedient morality	*Tough, stretching moral practices*
Reaction to symptoms	*Proaction dealing with cause*
Disparate actions	*Unifying team actions*
Compensation based on actions and personal characteristics	*Compensation based on positive performance*
Fragmentation and diffusion of effort	*Purpose and direction*
Getting	*Giving*
Focusing on weaknesses	*Building on strengths*
Commitment to self only	*Commitment to goals and objectives that transcend self*
Guarded behavior	*Caring and giving*
Negative listening	*Positive listening*
Dis-satisfaction (past oriented)	*Un-satisfaction (future oriented)*
Dissent	*Protest*
"Gamesmanship"	*Accountability for results*
Expecting the worst	*Expecting the best*
Pushing, driving	*Leading*
Grim	*Cheerful*
Negative G forces	*Positive G forces* [see next chapter]

I warned the seminar participants, "As you examine these transitions, be prepared for some fairly drastic changes. They are tough and they require work, but the rewards for truly tough-minded managers are enormous."

At the end of the day my new friend, Ann, came up to shake hands. "This was not at all what I expected and I'm glad it wasn't. This kind of *lifestyle and managerial style is tough, all right, but I know it's going to be fun, too."*

Five years later, in another part of the country, I was waiting in the airport for my flight when I heard a buoyant voice call out, "Hey, Joe, do you remember me?" I turned around and barely recognized the bright and vital woman walking toward me. Of course, you've guessed who it was. Ann and I sat down over a cup of coffee and she poured out a heartening story.

She had moved up three levels in her organization and had just been interviewed for a major executive position in another company. She stressed that making the tough-minded transition had not been easy. She'd encountered many rocks and shoals. She pointed out, however, that these happenings had only strengthened her because, as she said, "I had a dream and I learned to build muscles and action steps into that dream."

I asked her what the single most significant insight had been. Her answer was unhesitating: "Understanding the difference between a hard *mind and a* tough *mind. It started all the other things happening."*

She had copied down the verbatim definition of tough-mindedness from the seminar and had become familiar with the real meaning of tough, as follows:

WHAT "TOUGH" REALLY MEANS

If I place two pieces of material the same size, shape and form on an anvil, and one is made of granite, the other of leather, and then hit each with a hammer, what will happen? The granite will shatter into pieces, precisely *because* it is hard. It is rigid, brittle, and weak. The leather is barely dented, precisely because it is *not* hard. It is flexible, malleable, resilient, elastic, durable, supple—and it is *tough!*

"It became a real thrill," she said, "to continuously seek to open, strengthen, stretch, and toughen my mind. Another thrill was to discover that real *assertiveness meant 'the logical exposition and deployment of my strengths.' It certainly helped me to ultimately understand how much more we get when we give from a strength-based level of self-esteem and confidence."*

Ann has continued to grow and is now heading a major division of people who themselves are growing because of her strong, caring, and tough-minded leadership. Her income is far beyond her earlier dreams. She is using one of the world's most underused resources—womanpower—with courage, commitment, enthusiasm, tough-mindedness, and action. She has begun to lead.

PERFORMANCE IS ALL THAT MATTERS

To declare that performance is all that matters sounds a little rigid and unbending at first. The term *performance*, after all, means "getting it done"! Buck Rodgers, the charismatic leader who was vice-president of marketing at IBM, puts it well in his book, *Getting the Best Out of Yourself and Others:*

> *Motivating another person to attain success is anything but an act of altruism. If you are an executive or in management, you have responsibility to the people you manage—and the company you work for—to motivate others to grow, to improve, and to flourish. You want them to produce more, waste less, and be more innovative.*[1]

Right about here it would be a good idea to do a little soul searching. You must decide what you expect the performance of your team members to yield. In other words, why are you in business? What are your goals?

☐ To acquire a condo? A sports car?
☐ To produce a greater return on investment?
☐ To actualize your possibilities as an individual?
☐ To increase your net profit?
☐ To create new things?
☐ To improve service to consumers?
☐ To market a better product?
☐ To bring in new customers?
☐ To provide leadership?
☐ To build a personal estate?
☐ To enhance your lifestyle and that of others?
☐ To retire at an early age?
☐ To turn leadership over to younger people?
☐ To develop a corporate image?
☐ To transform organizations and lives?

It is essential that the tough-minded interpretation of *performance* be fully understood. Performance means the *total* performance of the person and includes as much emphasis on qualitative measures of performance as the quantitative. Real and satisfying quantitative results simply will not happen without a high, even excellent, measure of qualitative indices such

1. (New York: Harper & Row, 1987).

as commitment, confidence, courage, integrity, personal renewal, loyalty, hard work, fairness, judgment, and uncommonly good common sense.

Do you love and respect the dignity and worth of your team members enough to truly integrate this into every dimension of your organization? Every level of the "P" pyramid? Do you *care* enough?

PERFORMANCE, JAPANESE STYLE

The chairman of Mitsubishi was once interviewed on the subject of lifetime employment in Japanese industries. "What do you do if a middle manager starts misperforming?" he was asked. "What do you do with him, given that you're committed to employ him for a lifetime?"

The chairman said quickly, "Oh, that's a problem we've studied a great deal. First, we check out the situation to find if there's something we could change to improve his performance. But, if we really don't understand why he's performing badly, we promote him. Because in 72.4 percent (or thereabouts) of the times we promote someone, their performance immediately improves."

Action Steps for Increasing Performance

1. Ask *everybody* in the organization to submit ideas and suggestions in sculpting the best possible mission, philosophy, and broad goals.
2. Develop clear and specific standards of performance.
3. Relate all compensation and perquisites directly to performance.
4. Dismantle rigid, hierarchical compensation systems and take bold leaps in policy and procedure to ensure that all team members are rewarded generously for measurable contribution to the fulfillment of the customer's needs.
5. Provide in-depth understanding by all team members that the awesome possibilities of computers are totally dependent on the strength, focus, and application of human *minds*. Computers are potent tools—but only tools.
6. Expect the best—and *reinforce* it.

CHAPTER 4

REVERSE THE G FORCES—
PIVOTAL LEADERSHIP

*Old habits have tremendous pull. Breaking deeply
imbedded habits of procrastination, criticism,
overeating or oversleeping involves more than a little
will power. We may be dealing with basic character
issues and need achieve some basic reorientation or
transformation.*

STEPHEN R. COVEY, OWNER AND PUBLISHER,
EXECUTIVE EXCELLENCE

Most of the current approaches to training and development are bankrupt. We must make a major break with the past. From push to pull, from static to dynamic, from compression to expansion—that's the wave of the future! Splendid new possibilities are opening in all directions, and the latent creative energy lurking in the average human mind is truly awesome.

Just one example of these myriad possibilities is the networking and communication power of computers. All growth, all development will depend completely on the *quality of the minds* of current and potential leaders. In *The Effective Executive* (1966), Peter Drucker—as usual—says it well:

> *All [a computer] can do is compute. For this reason, it demands clear analysis, especially of the boundary conditions the decision has to satisfy. And that requires risk-taking judgment of a high order.*[1]

In other words, the computer can amplify and liberate minds of leaders for their real jobs—thinking, leading, and optimizing resources.

POSITIVE AND NEGATIVE G FORCES

What is a G force, anyway? "G" stands for gravity, and is a term scientists use as a unit of measure, to describe the amount of the force exerted on Earth by gravity. I use the term figuratively, and in this figurative sense there are both negative and positive G forces. Negative G forces are the self-defeating habits of the past—passivity, focus on weaknesses, "driving" attitudes; they only pull us down. Positive G forces of the future are the passionate attitudes and practices that energize us. In a sense, these G forces pull us *up* (even though we all know that literal gravity cannot); see Figure 4.1. This chapter—indeed, this entire book—is about how to release yourself from the negative G forces of the past and plug into the positive G forces of the future.

CYBERNETIC CIRCLE OF LEADERSHIP

Twelve key requirements—positive G forces—for the tough-minded visioneer of the future are displayed in Figure 4.2, which is called the cybernetic circle of leadership. What the mind of man can conceive, the dedicated and focused energy of man can achieve. The quest for the new and better requires tough-minded leaders to study and master these twelve steps.

Step 1. Clarify Purpose and Direction

In "Tapping Into the New Sources of Power" (*Executive Excellence*, February 1988), Alan Posner and Barry Randolph write:

> *Leaders are expected to be forward-looking, to have a sense of direction, and to be concerned about the future of the enterprise. Followers want to have a feeling for the destination that the leader has in mind.*

1. (New York: Harper & Row, Publishers, Inc.).

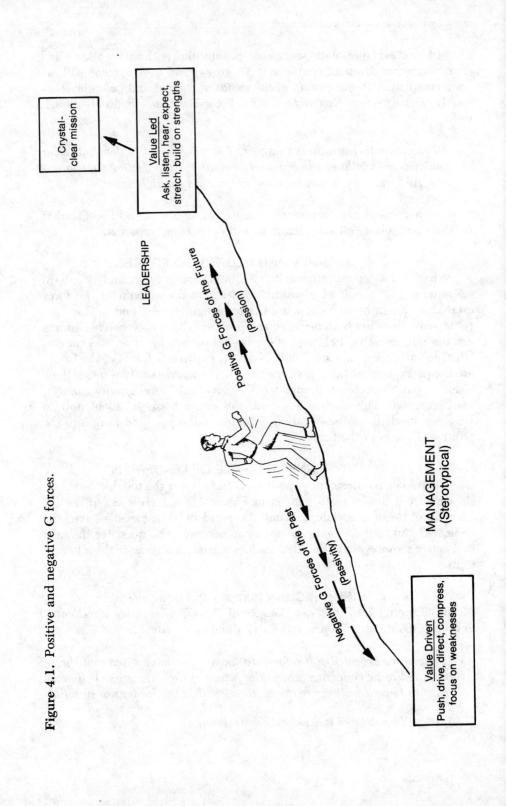

Figure 4.1. Positive and negative G forces.

Figure 4.2. The cybernetic circle of leadership.

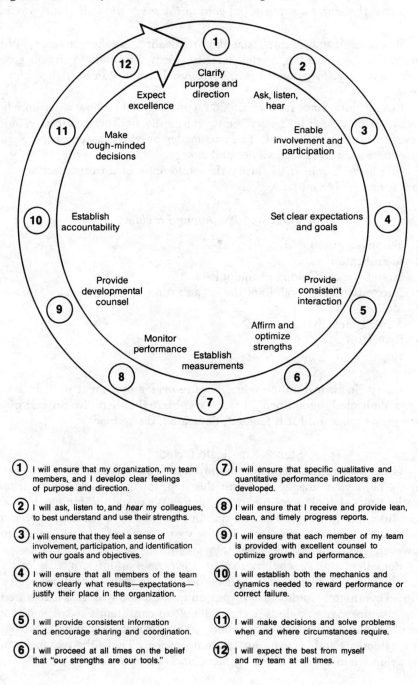

(1) I will ensure that my organization, my team members, and I develop clear feelings of purpose and direction.

(2) I will ask, listen to, and *hear* my colleagues, to best understand and use their strengths.

(3) I will ensure that they feel a sense of involvement, participation, and identification with our goals and objectives.

(4) I will ensure that all members of the team know clearly what results—expectations—justify their place in the organization.

(5) I will provide consistent information and encourage sharing and coordination.

(6) I will proceed at all times on the belief that "our strengths are our tools."

(7) I will ensure that specific qualitative and quantitative performance indicators are developed.

(8) I will ensure that I receive and provide lean, clean, and timely progress reports.

(9) I will ensure that each member of my team is provided with excellent counsel to optimize growth and performance.

(10) I will establish both the mechanics and dynamics needed to reward performance or correct failure.

(11) I will make decisions and solve problems when and where circumstances require.

(12) I will expect the best from myself and my team at all times.

Where are we going? What will it be like there? The leader's clarity about the target objectives [is] akin to the magnetic pull of a compass.

It is difficult to overemphasize the practicality, the sheer necessity, of a dream that provides lift, stretch, clarity, focus, and pull. A dream gives voltage, vitality, focus, and joy to our days. It is the stuff of high achievement.

Leaders must have followers, and no one can truly follow a person who has no dream. Such a "leader" must constantly improvise directives and orders—G forces of the past. The *true* leader provides shared purpose and direction fueled by shared values and energy.

The leader's role is to clarify the philosophy of an organization and state it succinctly and powerfully.

Company Philosophy Provides

☐ Vision—a grand design
☐ Identification
☐ Stretch—a quickening of the pulse
☐ Integration of the values of the organization
☐ Motives
☐ A spirit that lifts
☐ Positivism
☐ Hope

Harry Emerson Fosdick said, "No life ever grows great until it is focused, dedicated, disciplined." I will paraphrase that here: No *organization* ever grows great until it is focused, dedicated, disciplined.

Step 2. Ask, Listen, Hear

Great leaders *pull* the team forward and keep it on course. It is so easy for the old-style manager to dismiss this step, to cop out and say, "I listen all the time—I took a course in listening." We're calling for much more than listening, however. The real question is, do you *hear?* If you *listen* to your team members, you'll perceive the words they use. If you *hear* them, however, you'll understand what they *mean.*

Retooling your vocabulary so that it expresses an interrogative leadership style rather than a directive or declarative style cannot be accomplished overnight. Confidence in your uniqueness and strengths is required. The insecure manager finds it very difficult to consistently ask, listen, and *hear* because of a lifetime spent subtly and subconsciously building defensive statements and "cover your tail" approaches. That's the reason for all the defensive memos, meeting agendas, and correspondence we see.

Figure 4.3. Top-down organization of the past.

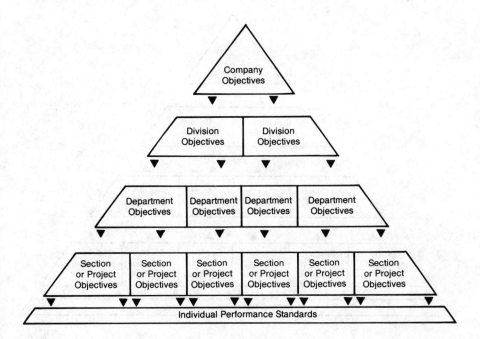

Tough-minded and *truly confident* leaders are able to develop and maintain emotional vulnerability, the capacity to let others in and let themselves out. This enables them to move beyond *dialogue*, which means two or more people engaged in monologues, to *communication*, which means shared meaning with shared understanding. The G forces of the future will require in-depth commitment to these deep levels of personal growth and change. The payoff can be enormous.

> *If I can listen to what he tells me. If I can*
> *understand how it seems to him, if I can sense the*
> *emotional flavor which it has for him then I will be*
> *releasing potent forces of change within him.*
> PSYCHOLOGIST CARL ROGERS

Step 3. Enable Involvement and Participation

The whole concept of the corporation must change if involvement and participation of all team members are to become realities. Please note that in Figure 4.3, the traditional flow of directiveness goes *down* from the top. Edicts are issued. Directives are propounded. The will of management is

Figure 4.4. Bottom-up organization of the future.

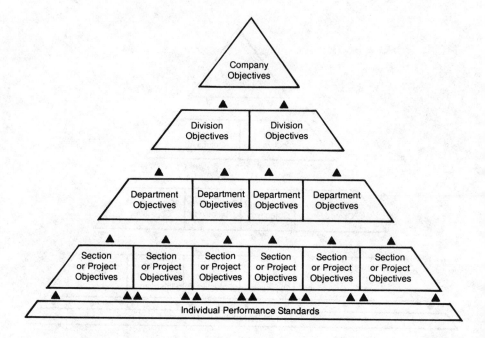

externally imposed on the organization. In Figure 4.4, energy and effort flow upward; they are lifted, pulled, and *expected* rather than pushed, pressed, and *directed*. Benefits are many. For example:

- ☐ Team members feel significant, listened to, valued as individuals.
- ☐ They feel they had a hand in something bigger than themselves.
- ☐ They feel some emotional investment in "their plan."
- ☐ They have enhanced feelings of belonging, opportunity, security, recognition, and, above all, significance.
- ☐ They will expend more energy and *work harder and smarter* to meet and fulfill the new expectations.

Step 4. Set Clear Expectations and Goals

The goals of the company—what it is expected to achieve—are the responsibility of its leader. Do you know the answers to these questions?

- ☐ *What* are the expectations of your customers, publics, or constituencies? Do you know? It is crucial to find out.

☐ *Where* do they expect their needs to be met? Where do you expect to fulfill them?

☐ *Who* is your market? Do you really know? Have you truly assessed your consumer motivations and expectations?

☐ *How* should these constituencies be best served? Have you mobilized the best data and ideas from your staff?

☐ *Why* are you in business? Do you actually know precisely the basic utility you are ostensibly organized to serve? What is it?

☐ *When*, at what targeted intervals, will these questions be addressed and resolved?

In a very real sense, the leader's expectations determine the future of the organization. People tend to deliver what is expected of them—be it good or bad. If you encountered a team member in the shop, factory, or office, and that person asked, "What do you expect from me?" would you have an answer? Now suppose that person also asked, "What do you expect from *your* job? What do you expect from the future?" Could you explain your goals?

Step 5. Provide Consistent Interaction

There is enormous value in "leading by walking around" *if* you know what to do and *say* as you walk around. I emphasize *say* because interaction is really communication, and words are our most sophisticated and practical tools of communication. Here is a comprehensive list of *directive* actions, words, and concepts—negative G forces—to avoid:

Language of the Past

Push	Secondary purpose
Tell	Defensiveness and rote
Input	Caution
Compress	*Dissatisfaction*
Intended to guide	"I *want* you to . . ."
Repress	Maintenance or erosion of motivation
Suppress	*Directed* accountability
Depress	Invulnerable
Advise	Defensive
Impact	Discontinuity
Comply	Inconsistent motivation
Implode	Resistance
Contract	Expedience
Rigidity	"Do as I say . . ."

Language of the Past

Inward and down	Inflict motive on others
Static	Autocracy
Blunt	Cynicism
Centripetal	Theory X
Replication of	Forgetting
creativity	Resentful
Anxieties	Compel
Repressed and glossed	Concern for active *compliance*
conflict	Retardation
Manipulated	Early obsolescence
Resignation	Reduce
Robotlike	Couldn't
Can't	Wouldn't
Don't	Didn't
Won't	Shouldn't

Did you find any "pull" in any of these words?

Note, please, that the *recipient* of these actions and words feels directed, diminished, and, all too often, emotionally drowned.

Now here is a list of *expective* words, actions, and concepts—positive G forces. Absorb them, understand them, and *use* them as you walk around and lead.

Language of the Future

Commit to	Count on
Look forward	Prospective and perspective
Hope	Future-oriented
Await	Predict
Evoke	Promise
Unfold	Ask
Grow	Create
Blossom	Enthusiasm
Anticipate	Primary purpose
Pull	Vulnerability and openness
Lead	Care
Output	*Un*satisfied
Lift	"Will you . . . ?"
Counsel	Motive-action
Expand	Accountability
Explode	Give
Outward and up	Share

Language of the Future

Dynamic	Confront
Eager	"Follow me"
Impatient and/or patient	The "we" feeling
Foresee	Sense of wonder
Prepare for	Build
Envision	Forgiving
Apprehend	Take aim
Target	Empathic
Catalytic action	Concern for results
Candor	Solves conflict
Surface conflict	Release
Stimulate	Sensing
Respect	Renewal
Reciprocal response	Exploration
Reassurance of dignity	Attract

I urge you to study and use the *expective* words as you replace and displace *directive* words. Truly, you become what you *say!*

Step 6. Affirm and Optimize Strengths

In their book *Leaders* (1985), Warren Bennis and Burt Nanus say:

For the most part, the leaders emphasized their strengths and tended to soft pedal or minimize their weaknesses. Which is not to say that they weren't aware of personal weaknesses but rather that they didn't harp on them. . . . Recognizing strengths and compensating for weaknesses represent the first step in achieving positive self-regard.[2]

Tough-minded visioneers know that the only reality of a person is the sum of his or her strengths.

Here is a definition of leadership for the turbulent decade ahead:

Leadership: Development of a clear and complete system of expectations in order to identify, evoke, and use the strengths of all resources in the organization—the most important of which is *people*.

All great organizations of the future will create and develop a computerized strengths bank that can be accessed in a great variety of situations. With this powerful tool at hand, the new organizational dictum called "the

2. (New York: Harper & Row, Publishers, Inc.).

logical deployment of strengths" becomes not only a day-by-day but an hour-by-hour reality.

The strengths-centered leader is better equipped to provide confident, calm, rational, and stretching expectations—and to set the pace!

Step 7. Establish Measurements

Increasingly in the Age of the Mind, indices of performance will be *qualitative*, even as we develop increasingly accurate and sophisticated methods of developing bottom-line numbers that are projective and stretching. I'm saying here that leadership must be *subjective* even as the measurements of performance become increasingly *objective*. Over the years, I have heard many executives say earnestly, "I must be more objective." In reality, leaders must increasingly concentrate on *subjective* human qualities, and use the objective data, tools, and instruments as aids in determining precise measurements.

Step 8. Monitor Performance

"Activity" reports are out; "progress reports" are in. Accurate, realistic progress reports can work effectively only within the infrastructure of

Mission→Philosophy→Goals→Objectives→Action Plans→ and Performance Standards.

These progress reports should be future oriented, focusing on actual results rather than on activity. They should be lean, succinct, and cogent. Winston Churchill required that *every* report or major recommendation be distilled into one page. The discipline required for such focus, brevity, and relevance is a powerful developmental device in itself, and, of course, frees the next higher reporting level executive to function much more effectively.

You should always follow these key guidelines when preparing progress reports:

☐ State your purpose.
☐ Promote system and sequence.
☐ Pay attention to order and flow.
☐ Consider impact on service and profit.
☐ Make sure that the objectives and plans are conducive to effective decision making.

Monitoring performance through performance appraisals in the new leadership climate requires thoughtful and thorough meshing of both mechanics and dynamics, as illustrated in Figure 4.5.

Figure 4.5. Performance appraisal: Meshing expectations to optimize performance.

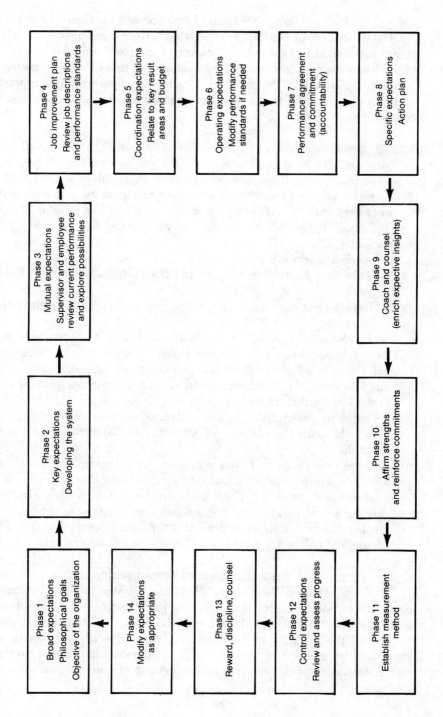

Step 9. Provide Development Counsel

Just as leaders of the future know that setting performance standards means more than just establishing objective numbers, they know too that evaluating a team member's performance means more than just matching numbers against goals. Tough-minded leaders view performance appraisals as a rich opportunity for teaching and counseling. Here are seven rules for conducting an effective appraisal:

1. *Give feedback.* Frequent communication ensures that there will be no surprises! Frequent communication and feedback on the job help overcome fear during the actual performance appraisal.
2. *Evaluate your* own *performance before you evaluate the team member's performance.* Are you responsible for his or her good or bad performance? If you point a finger, are you aware of the three pointing back at you?
3. *Schedule a warmup period:*
   a. Take time to develop rapport and discuss the advantage of the appraisal.
   b. Review the information on hand to measure the team member's performance.
4. *Be candid and specific.* Get right to the point in discussing a team member's performance on the job. Honesty, candor, and responsiveness will result in a big payoff for you and the team member.
5. *Build on strengths.* This tough-minded approach enables team members to work toward their greatest potential. Team members must use their strengths to accomplish a job; they cannot use weaknesses since weaknesses are only the *absence* of strengths or insufficiently developed strengths.
6. *Be a positive listener.* Listen with ears, eyes, heart, and your entire being. Nonverbal communication often says more than words.
7. *Evaluate and appraise* performance, *not the person.* Evaluate the team member's performance and end results. Don't judge the person. Judgments come from a focus on weaknesses. Evaluations are based on identifying and enhancing strengths—the stuff of *empowerment.*

Step 10. Establish Accountability

In *Tough-Minded Management,* I stated that accountability means the clear, warm understanding that you do a job or get out of it. This is even more true as a stabilizing truth for the last decades of the twentieth century.

Before the negative or punitive portion of the whole-balanced and tough-minded concept of accountability is enforced, it places a premium on the excellence of the example and leadership of *you.* I'll deal with that here, but first, let me clear up the notion that accountability is primarily negative. It is not!

Accountability provides first of all for rewards for outstanding performance. Only when the desired level of performance clearly cannot be reached does the tough-minded leader take punitive steps.

In "Tapping Into the New Sources of Power" (*Executive Excellence*, February 1988), Alan Posner and Barry Randolph write:

> *Coercive power is based on the perception that another person has the ability to punish or withhold valued resources. Effective executives avoid using coercive power except when absolutely necessary because its use creates resentment and erodes their personal power base. With coercion there is no chance of gaining commitment.*

If you are a truly tough-minded expective leader, you will recognize that organizational authority is to be used as the last rather than the first expedient. Before considering termination or demotion, you will make sure you have provided the team member with:

- [ ] The right example
- [ ] The what, where, when, who, how, and why of his or her job expectations
- [ ] The information, training, materials, and resources needed
- [ ] Clear insight into his or her present and potential strengths—congenial facts
- [ ] A clear assessment of his or her personal possibilities
- [ ] Enhanced understanding of his or her uniqueness or value
- [ ] Above all, warm clarity of expectation
- [ ] Clearly communicated agreement as to the time frame involved in shaping up or shipping out

A truly tough-minded leader will perceive that pure organizational authority is a poor substitute for *real* authority—the authority of example.

Step 11. Make Tough-Minded Decisions

Modern tough-minded leaders who are plugged into the G forces of the future believe in and practice consultive decision making. That means they:

1. Provide excellent training and example for team members, so that they know the what, where, when, who, how, and why of their jobs and the organization.

2. Expect completed staff work. Team members do not bring their problems to managers. Rather, they do the research, thinking, and preparation they are paid for, and then present the manager with appropriate proposals and recommendations. In this way, leaders can truly manage by expectation and can make full use of the skills for which team members are paid. Of course the managers are in a position to reject, modify, or accept the proposal.
3. Listen carefully, solicit the best input and suggestions from appropriate team members, and make the decision only if it is inappropriate for the team member to do so.
4. Make the decision (if they should) with full awareness of their accountability for its success.
5. Strive always to push decisions down the level where they should most properly be made. Unit leaders strive to back the decisions of their team members firmly, consistently, and fairly. They expect team members to provide the same type of support to them.

In short, before making major decisions, leaders strive consistently to use the wisdom and resources available—and then they do three crucial things:

1. Ask
2. Listen
3. Hear

Making decisions is what leaders are *paid* for!

Step 12. Expect Excellence and *Reinforce* It

☐   Do you care enough about you and your team to put some *muscle* into your dreams?

☐   Do you care enough to gradually build up reserves and emotional files— mental and spiritual stamina?

☐   Do you care enough to define yourself?

☐   Do you care enough to *confront* your hopes?

☐   Do you care enough to ask much from your life and from your team?

☐   Do you care enough to build "forgiving" relationships?

☐   Do you care enough to seek strengths in all things?

☐   Do you care enough to replace cynicism with wonder?

☐   Do you care enough to eliminate words like can't, don't, and won't (what I call the lousy apostrophe-t's) from your vocabulary?

☐   Do you care enough to share the real you with others?

☐ Do you care enough to distinguish between tranquility (the bland leading the bland) and *real* happiness: passionate confrontation of life's possibilities?

☐ Do you care enough to lead?

☐ Do you care enough to expect the best?

If you care that much, you *can* and *will* reverse the G forces. Plugging into the G forces of the future requires rigorous assessment of, and probably change in, our appetites and passions, pride and pretensions, aspirations and ambitions. The tough-minded leader of the future will settle for nothing less.

Remember, the size of your dream will determine the size of the person you will become.

CHAPTER **5**

A *NEW* "SYSTEMS" APPROACH
TO MANAGEMENT

The key to success in the Integrated Planning Process lies in getting the involvement and commitment of everyone in the organization. Remember, the purpose of planning is not to produce plans; it is to produce results, and this requires total organization and commitment.

GEORGE L. MORRISEY, *THE EXECUTIVE GUIDE TO STRATEGIC PLANNING*

We have heard a great deal in recent years about the "systems" approach to management. Many definitions of the term *system* are offered by its proponents, including:

"A group of interacting bodies under the influence of related forces."
"The body considered as a functional unit."

"An organized set of doctrines, ideas, or principles usually intended to explain the arrangement or working of a systematic whole."
"Harmonious arrangement or pattern."
"An assemblage of substances that is in or tends to equilibrium."

Sounds great, doesn't it? Unfortunately, many people—and I am one—believe that the systems approach, on the whole, has not worked well. One of the principal reasons this approach has not delivered its full payload is that it has been thought of as a detached, "scientific" way of doing things. In this regard, consider these ideas:

☐ A good management organization *is* a system.
☐ A poor management organization is also a system, but a *poor* one.
☐ A key weakness in systems, and therefore in management development, has been the tendency to view a system simply as an aggregate of materials, of diagrams, flowcharts, data-based modules, equipment, and other nonhuman resources.
☐ A true system, whether a leadership system or any other kind, is a gestalt, a blend of functionally compatible components.
☐ A system is really a system of *values*, a combination of essential truths. Values are the subjective interpretation of the immutable laws of the universe that shape and guide human reactions.

The orderly expression and transfer of tough-minded values into practices is the essential process involved in building a climate of productivity. It is a dynamic interweaving of individual behavior patterns that produce group accomplishment greater than the sum of its parts. An excellent symphony orchestra is a *system* of music.

The system, then, should be conceived as an orderly juxtaposition of resources (people, money, material, time, and space) blended to fulfill expectations of, by, about, and for *people*. This is my central focus.

What we have, then, is a *new* kind of systems approach, focused on expectations. In short, we replace MBO (management by objectives) with MBE—management by expectations.

MBE: MANAGEMENT BY EXPECTATIONS

The ongoing effectiveness and possible excellence of this system depends completely on in-depth understanding and consistent application of the three principles embodied in the cybernetic circle of operational effectiveness (see Figure 5.1). Commitment leads to conviction, which leads to involvement, which in turn leads to renewed commitment—and the circle continues.

Figure 5.1. The cybernetic circle of operational effectiveness.

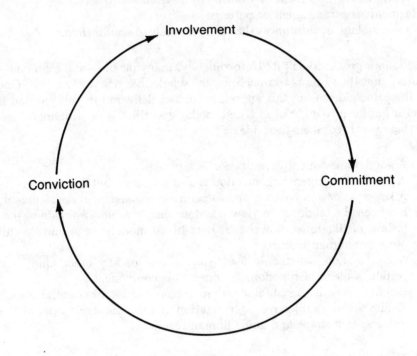

In countless instances throughout the country, our consulting team has seen meticulously prepared plans go awry simply because the people in the organization did not feel sufficiently *involved* (ask, listen, hear) to make a truly visceral *commitment* that could be carried out with *conviction*.

For outstanding involvement, commitment, and conviction to become reality, you must make sure all team members feel:

☐ Significant
☐ Listened to and heard.
☐ Empowered and valued
☐ Consistently informed
☐ Rewarded in all suitable ways
☐ Like winners

Above all, you must create a climate where all team members experience shared meaning, shared understanding, shared vision, and shared values.

A SYSTEM OF EXPECTIVE LEADERSHIP

To get down to specifics, in Figure 5.2 I have attempted to present an overall expective leadership system. Let us discuss each of the key elements in turn.

Phase 1: Research

Organizational research should be considered as a here-and-now kind of event as well as an ongoing process. The needs of the total organization must be continually viewed against external conditions in the country and in the world that will affect what happens in the organization. The connection is now all too clear between factors that were once thought to be unconnected. The six phases that follow must be carefully thought through in terms of the expectations of the people employed by the organization.

Phase 2: Plan

For some time now, planning—particularly long-range planning—has been a popular topic of conversation in management circles. Every progressive executive believes in planning; you can no more knock it than you can apple pie, the Constitution, or motherhood.

Unfortunately, in my view, they believe in the wrong *kind* of planning. I am firmly convinced that the kind of dynamic, responsive, and resilient planning needed in the turbulent years ahead must be something like 90 percent emphasis on human dynamics and 10 percent emphasis on procedural mechanics or processes.

The number of organizations that have not clearly defined their business mission is surprising. They have never bothered to ask, "Why are we in business?" (or, for a nonprofit organization, "Why do we exist?"). Another way of phrasing this all-important question is "What is the basic utility we are geared to deliver?"

And what, pray tell, does that have to do with planning? The whole purpose of strategic and tactical planning is to calculate future market needs for this basic utility and to make provision and decisions to fulfill these expectations.

Don't wait to start your planning program. If you hold back until you are meticulously prepared in every detail to establish magnificent objectives, let's face it—you'll never get started. The important thing is to set your goals and get the planning machinery under way. You must, of course, be impatient with your plans and their progress. But you won't have anything to refine and improve if you don't make a beginning.

Where do you begin? With a thoroughly fortified knowledge of your consumer. Time and again, companies have built a product and then—and only then—set out to determine who wanted it and how to distribute it. This is asking for disaster. Base all your plans directly or indirectly on a

Figure 5.2. A system of leadership by expectations.

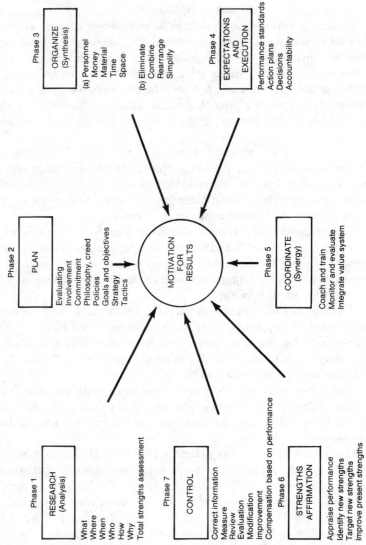

Phase 3

ORGANIZE
(Synthesis)

(a) Personnel
Money
Material
Time
Space

(b) Eliminate
Combine
Rearrange
Simplify

Phase 4

EXPECTATIONS
AND
EXECUTION

Performance standards
Action plans
Decisions
Accountability

Phase 2

PLAN

Evaluating
Involvement
Commitment
Philosophy, creed
Policies
Goals and objectives
Strategy
Tactics

MOTIVATION
FOR
RESULTS

Phase 5

COORDINATE
(Synergy)

Coach and train
Monitor and evaluate
Integrate value system

Phase 1

RESEARCH
(Analysis)

What
Where
When
Who
How
Why
Total strengths assessment

Phase 7

CONTROL

Correct information
Measure
Review
Evaluation
Modification
Improvement
Compensation based on performance

Phase 6

STRENGTHS
AFFIRMATION

Appraise performance
Identify new strengths
Target new strengths
Improve present strengths

well-researched fund of data, a never-ending hunger, about *what* the consumers want, *where* they want it, *when* they want it, *who* they are, *how* they want it, and—above all—*why* they want it. Imaginative closed-loop systems of customer information input, retrieval, and use are imperative.

Your other main source of inspiration for the plan is your own people. Modern tough-minded leaders know they can gain additional insights, hunches, clues, and hard data from their entire team if they exert the self-control and discipline needed to truly tap their expectations. Leaders know they are accountable for the decisions implicit in the job but want the best and most realistic future-oriented ideas they can get. Above all, modern executives need *vision*—both macro and micro.

The overall conceptual schema for strategic planning is shown in Figure 5.3. Because of the excellent current books on strategic planning, I have deliberately omitted additional elaboration on these key components. The need for more complete detail in these areas should be implicit in the tough-minded leaders' assumptions. The books of George Morrisey are particularly recommended for this purpose.

Phase 3: Organize

The whole lexicon of organizational terms and concepts must change significantly in the context of the total tough-minded leadership approach to the turbulent decade ahead. My premise is that since *the logical deployment of strengths* is the organizational paradigm for the future, the following seven questions are crucial:

1. Can you truly perceive present and potential strengths in functional design?
2. Can you truly perceive present and potential strengths in assessing your team members?
3. Can you fit the parts together in such a way that you create not only a logical synthesis but also a symbiotic and synergistic whole?
4. Does every function make a discernible and measurable contribution to objectives, goals, and philosophy?
5. Will the new organization lend itself to perpetuity and stability?
6. Is there sufficient balance of functions and personalities to constitute a true team?
7. Finally, does your key criterion ensure that the organization lends itself to blended expectations?

Phase 4: Expectations and Execution

In Figure 5.4, we see some of the real nuts and bolts of expective management. Clear definition of the assignment must be effectively (and concurrently) delegated and communicated in such a way that team members

Figure 5.3. Strategic planning process.

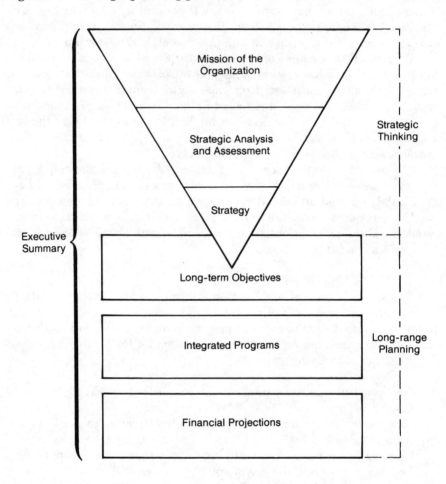

understand the what, where, when, who, how, and why in the specific context of their jobs, and in relation to the standards of performance expected.

Team members' understanding of the results you expect—their accountability—should be so thorough that you can exercise full release and trust. Of course, hand in hand with that trust goes feedback: you must receive performance information in the form and at the intervals you expect. Consultive decision making is an exercise in democracy, wisdom, and practicality. It provides the involvement that leads to commitment and conviction (take another look at Figure 5.1 earlier in this chapter).

This kind of interactive decision making also allows you to get the best

Figure 5.4. Designing functional assignments.

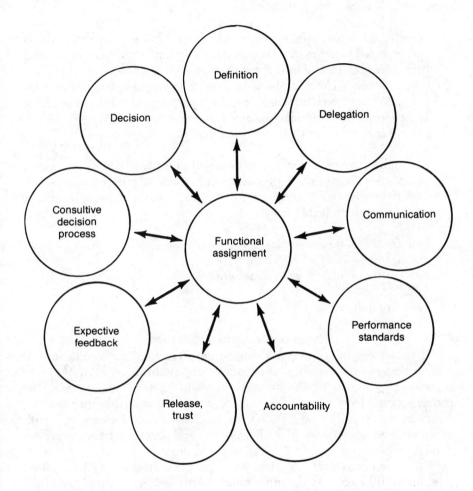

information possible from your team to help make sound decisions. In sum, it requires that you analyze the alternatives, balance the benefits, and calculate the contingencies.

To effectively carry out the elements in Phase 4, you will need a sound understanding of all that has been discussed in this book.

Phase 5: Coordination (Synergize)

Expective coaching is the wave of the future. I believe we can confidently expect to see new research, insights, and techniques in this area. It is crucial if we are to achieve optimum coordination.

For team members to experience a positive and developmental coaching experience, it is important that they:

☐ Perceive the what, where, when, who, how, and why of their present and expected performance. It is particularly important that team members understand the *why*—the stuff of real motivation.
☐ Feel a strong identification with overall goals, objectives, and standards. Without such a feeling, nothing approaching optimum coaching and coordination will take place.
☐ Believe that their strengths are what you value about them.

Remember, people's total value—current and potential—is the sum of the values they exemplify. To focus on individual or group weaknesses is not only *un*productive, it is *counter*productive, because it tends to rigidify behavior into nonmalleable fragments.

You are the sum of your strengths.
You are the sum of your values.
You are the sum of your expectations.
AND
They are indivisible!

Phase 6: Strengths Affirmation

If we believe that a person's deepest need is a need for significance, it follows that our own feelings of significance grow in direct relationship to a growing awareness of our strengths as leaders and as total people. The converse also is true. When we search for, dwell on, and reiterate a person's weakness, we stultify that person's possibilities, reduce feelings of significance, inhibit growth on and off the job, and seriously hamper performance.

To overemphasize the weaknesses of people is to shackle them with a miserable self-image. On the other hand, to strive diligently and truthfully and very consistently to help them know, understand, and *use* their strengths is to *set them free.*

Clear-eyed, objective, and consistent affirmation of strengths is one of the great pleasures for committed, expective leaders. They discover this adds zest and gusto to all their relationships—with their families and their team members as well.

Phase 7: Control

The term *control* conjures up visions of massive printouts, intimidating computer hardware and software, knitted brows, somber prognoses, and all the paraphernalia of a modern management information system (MIS).

And certainly these are important. No manager questions the value of a thoughtful system of budgets or profit plans. Much of the real value of a budget, however, is the painstaking analysis and study that precedes the actual figures.

I would like, in addition, to suggest that modern controls should meet two general sets of requirements. First, they should be:

Stretching
Economical
Meaningful
Appropriate
Timely
Simply stated and simple to operate

Second, it should be understood that the best of all controls is a fused, focused, loyal group of people who know:

☐ What is expected of them
☐ What they expect

Just as the whole concept of data-*driven* control must be relegated to the past, we must suffuse all new considerations of control with the terms customer-*led* and data-*responsive*. This becomes the basis for a badly needed overhaul of dated concepts of historical accounting. Remember the relatively obsolete *manager* manages *data*. The new *leader* leads *people*.

Above all, real control is a system of expectations, with calibrated checkpoints that indicate precisely how well the expectations are being met. Phase 7 flows into Phase 1 and the loop closes—a system of motivation for results, fueled and guided by expectations.

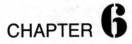

MASTERS OF STRENGTHS DEPLOYMENT

The strengths of an organization can be no stronger than the strengths of the personal relationships, the quality of the minds, and the strength of the shared values within it.

The only purpose of organization is to make one plus one equal three—or more. Two people must accomplish more than twice the work of one person or there is no organization! A new concept? Startling discovery? Hardly. This fundamental truth has been recognized for decades. It is the foundation of all systems of methods improvement, mass production, automation, and specialization.

In fact, there is a growing feeling today that we are nearing the end of the time of seeking increased efficiency through organization. Many sophisticated professionals—human resource specialists, professors, psychologists, and consultants—are preaching that the road to combined productive effort is through *dis*organization: using job enlargement, decentralization, task forces, matrix management, and unstructured social interaction.

Others believe that various permissive approaches are the answer. They advocate shared accountability, line-staff committees, junior boards, collective goal setting, and other so-called democratic processes. Some experts have completely given up trying to organize for greater human productivity and have turned to organizing machines instead of people.

All these "solutions" to the basic problem are superficial, piecemeal, disparate, patchwork, makeshift approaches that fall pitifully short of the breakthrough needed to realize the limitless and barely tapped potential of joint human effort.

A complete shift of emphasis must take place! Molding and manipulating people to achieve predefined patterns of behavior and dropping them into preconceived slots on an organization chart without regard for their individual strengths may make you feel powerful and important, but it is about as effective in achieving excellence as a square wheel. Compressing a person to fit a position that has been carefully interrelated to other positions (which in turn are filled by compressing other people) may be neat and orderly and will probably work moderately well—if you get rid of the people who won't stay compressed. Unfortunately, those are the people whose individuality you most need.

ORGANIZING BY STRENGTHS

The issue is clear: Do you want an organization with no loose ends? A box for everyone and everyone in his box? An organization where exceptions to the rule (even in the form of exceptional people who seldom follow the rules) are not allowed to exist, or at best only barely tolerated? An organization that runs moderately well, is moderately safe and secure, makes a moderate profit, enjoys moderate growth, and provides you and your team with a moderate degree of satisfaction and a moderate sense of achievement? If you prefer this approach, you need not feel guilty. Many do—and suffer no disgrace.

But you may want an organization that plugs into the G forces of the future, leads the parade, sets the pace in profit, growth, products, service, methods, and concepts; one that always seems able to come up with the breakthrough when it's needed; one that keeps its competitors so busy catching up they don't have time for anything else. If so, if you want to reap the rewards that justice dictates must always fall to the victor, you must make a fundamental decision: to expand people, not compress them, to build on their strengths, not focus on their weaknesses.

It isn't always easy. It requires weaving together a group of basically self-directed people, all doing what they do best, so as to achieve singleness of purpose and unity of direction. This, in turn, requires great artistry. Egalitarian teams, led by the first among equals, are the wave of tomorrow.

If, finally, you decide to strive for excellence and seek exceptional performance, then you must back your decision with demonstration, not just conversation, and begin building on strengths—starting with yourself. You also need to help your basically self-directed people realize that the one best way to grow as individuals is to build others constantly.

Organizing by strengths takes a lot of self-control and self-discipline. Be careful to include your own strengths along with those of your staff. You must be directly and deeply involved in the achievement of transcendent dreams and organizational objectives. Don't just sit back and oversee what is going on; use your own talents to accomplish specific tasks.

To develop these crucial qualities, we start with Phase 1 of the servo-system of strengths management (see Figure 6.1). Here we are applying this servo-system to the tough-minded manager as an *individual;* in Chapter 14 we'll use the servo-system with organizational operations.

AN EXERCISE FOR IDENTIFYING STRENGTHS

I have had the privilege of seeing some truly productive and beautiful things happen in client organizations to teams of all kinds and sizes when they begin to understand and practice systematic methods of strengths building. There are several methods for making this work; here's one I have used:

1. Seat your group in a circle (don't have more than twenty people).
2. Have them all (working individually) write down ten strengths they have identified in themselves.
3. Ask each person to look at each member of the group one at a time and mentally identify one significant strength in each person.
4. Starting at any point in the circle, choose the first subject. Ask the person on his or her left to name one significant strength about that person. Then proceed on around the circle until everyone has shared a strength-oriented perception of that person.
5. Move on to the second subject, then the third, and so on until everyone has had a turn. Provide whatever guidance is needed to keep the remarks totally positive and strength based. *No* negatives of any kind are permitted.

Every single person in a group of twenty hears nineteen strength-based comments about himself or herself from nineteen different personalities in nineteen different ways. Many people of even mature years may hear, for the first time, the kind of affirmation and reassurance most of us are hungry and thirsty for.

Figure 6.1. A servo-system of strengths management.

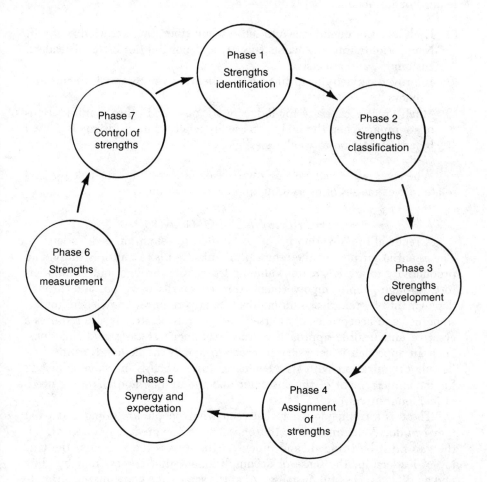

Another important bonus is that this is usually the first time people have ever been asked to identify, perceive, and articulate strengths—and *only* strengths—in anyone else. Now they are asked to do so *nineteen* times, and their minds literally start to reroute brain circuits. A vital process of renewal is underway.

At a seminar in Milwaukee I worked for one whole day on this exercise with forty company presidents. (Forty is really too large; smaller, more intimate groups are more effective.) At the end of the day they felt that they knew one another better than they did their own team members with whom they had worked many years.

This kind of group experience provides special, important benefits to a team. For instance:

- ☐ High levels of confidence and self-esteem; liberating knowledge of self.
- ☐ New insights into the wants, needs, and possibilities of team leaders, customers, and clients.
- ☐ Improved capacity to spring back resiliently from disappointments and setbacks.
- ☐ Much greater capacity for longer work days and other manifestations of stamina. When the body is basically healthy, most fatigue is caused by an orientation to weaknesses.

Whenever we dwell on our own weakness, we tend to look for and relate to weaknesses of everything and everyone around us.

THE RENEWAL ORGANIZATION

A renewal organization is one committed to tough-minded leadership. The essential purpose of the renewal organization is to multiply individual productivity to attain greater value-added results through joint human effort, through people empowerment, through clarity of vision, and through deployment of strengths. Building on strengths requires knowledge, understanding, and acceptance of yourself and your associates. It also requires a creative and flexible approach to the assignment of tasks and functions. Such an approach is necessary in order to match the demands of the new flexible organization with its ever-increasing emphasis on value-added Ps for the enhancement of the customer and the unique and changing needs of its human resources.

There is a tremendous gap between what people *are* doing and what they *can* do. We cannot jump this chasm with one great leap forward, but the gap must be bridged, and quickly. Doing so is the source of the true joy of leadership: the sense of accomplishment that comes from building and guiding a successful business and at the same time knowing the ultimate in human endeavor—building people and enhancing the customer.

Throughout this book, I am stressing the *primacy of people!* However, here is a perfect way to use the enormous capabilities of technology, particularly computers: to help us identify, classify, access, and use the strengths of our people. Computerized strengths banks will be at the heart of the style of leaders of the future.

Strength-based controls are liberating! I predict that the really fine organizations of the 1990s will select people for critical assignments by accessing their strengths banks, rather than relying on traditional criteria such as degrees, seniority, color, race, religion, appearance, job classifications, or what-have-you. Focused, laserlike deployment of strengths will ultimately become the norm.

BUILDING TEAM SYNERGY

Once strengths have been identified, you are well on your way to building powerful teams. Some key techniques and considerations for effective team building include the following steps:

1. Conduct sound and relevant research about wants, needs, and possibilities.
2. Take time to define what you want or expect to accomplish.
3. Set the example.
4. Allow for differences in the personalities, ambitions, and attitudinal sets of team members.
5. Develop consensus and unanimity.
6. Give steady feedback to provide progress data, recognition, and feelings of belonging and significance.
7. Stress the importance of each team member acquiring greater skill in asking legitimate, caring questions.
8. Be sure to teach and exemplify that a question is infinitely more powerful than a declarative statement in practical persuasiveness.
9. Seek to ensure the mutuality of motives and expectations of all members of the team.
10. Base all assignments on the logical deployment of strengths.

Finally, be aware that the excellent team has *tempo*, defined as "the speed with which an organization identifies problems and opportunities and makes and implements decisions." If you intend to meet the requirements of the turbulent decade, controls and effective team building must be indivisible.

Team building is something of a "hot" topic these days; we see articles and how-to advice almost everywhere we turn. But that doesn't mean it is easy. The forces that work against building strong teams are rampant. Some common ones include:

☐ The failure to realize that an objective, a motive, and an expective are virtually the same. Interpretations of the word *objective* have done much to shortchange the motivational possibilities inherent in it.

☐ Team members not understanding the what, where, when, who, how, and above all the *why* of their jobs and their organization.

☐ Lethargy, politicking, apathy, inefficiency, work of poor quality, and just plain lack of *caring* because "management" has not provided sufficient purpose and direction. There are thousands of "major managers" in this country today who will simply not be capable of rectifying such conditions in their organizational units unless they receive skilled counseling and development as individuals!

☐ Leaders who live, talk, and work in terms of what they are *against* instead of what they are *for*.

To instill the kind of vitality needed to fuel the vision, we need:

☐ A mutual feeling of *caring* about each other, a feeling that our colleagues and team members are walking bundles of uniqueness and strengths.

☐ The freedom to be emotionally vulnerable, open, and receptive to the wants, needs, problems, and *possibilities* of others.

☐ A reduced amount of "telling"—that is, abrasiveness, knee-jerk machismo, directiveness, pushing, and crowding. In contrast, take the word *tell* and turn it around so that it becomes *let*. I do not mean apathetic permissiveness. I mean letting team members feel involved, part of a strong, expectation-oriented approach.

☐ A strong, compelling example.

☐ A vital style and tone, one that comes from the chief executive officer through the chief operating officer and permeates the entire team.

☐ Clear and stretching expectations. This is one of the best possible ways to express your dedication and commitment to your team. I believe that when you care enough about a person to find out his or her best qualities, encourage these qualities, and *expect* commitment and conviction, you are demonstrating dedication, respect, and genuine affection.

☐ A lean headquarters and central staff; a sense of leanness throughout the entire organization.

☐ All the other elements described in the various cybernetic circles throughout this book.

CHAPTER

GREAT CHANGEMASTERS
ARE GREAT COMMUNICATORS

We rule the world by our words.
NAPOLEON BONAPARTE

In literally hundreds of seminars and workshops, and in hundreds of private counseling sessions with managers, my colleagues and I have sought to determine what is really at the core of the management job. After innumerable discussions, and after reviewing the results of numerous surveys, I have concluded that the total effectiveness of leaders rises or falls in direct proportion to their face-to-face communication skills—their interpersonal insights and actions.

What is the definition of communication? I have never had any member of a seminar audience who could give me the dictionary definition. And this is one of those instances where the definition of a word actually helps you perceive a lot of things about its meaning, its anatomy, and how to *do* it. We can define communication in four words:

Communication: *shared meaning, shared understanding.*

These four words, in a sense, say it all. Is there anything more we need for successful relationships? For successful family life? For successful job performance?

FACE-TO-FACE COMMUNICATION TOOLS

The tough, elusive elements that are found in truly effective one-to-one relationships are:

Vulnerability
Openness
Positive listening
Kinesics
High expectations
Avoiding judgments
Reinforcement
Caring
Integrity

Let's examine these elements one by one in the light of the statement that communication means "shared meaning, shared understanding."

Vulnerability

Real leaders—not those equipped with political, financial, or military power—have known for centuries that the courage to become and remain vulnerable in their relations with others requires strength and toughness. That kind of courage also *develops* strength.

Most of us know, on careful reflection, that the defensive, invulnerable person plateaus early in life in terms of growth, vitality, and the capacity to obtain "followership," without which a leader can't lead. Such a person ceases to act. And when we begin to *react* to people and events, we become static and rigid rather than flexible and responsive.

It is my belief that enlightened behavioral science research will increasingly prove that the confrontive requirements of vulnerability are vastly more developmental and effective than the avoidance expedient of invulnerability and defensiveness. Who grows when they flee? Who grows when they defend? Who grows when they covet safety and comfort?

A fundamental requirement for the leader who seeks this new, stretching attitude is a high measure of self-esteem. Years ago, I wrote in *Tough-*

Minded Management that real, sustaining self-confidence was the scarcest ingredient in managers. This still applies in full measure! It is the quintessential element of the fully functioning person.

It requires confidence, courage, and vulnerability to truly open up and feel *real interest* in what the other person is saying. It is when we stick our neck out, when we rally from rebuffs, failures, and insufficiencies, when we take risks in the human enterprise that we truly strengthen, toughen, and grow.

Openness

In a dictionary sense, *open* means "available, exposed, given access to, not covered." The capacity to achieve and maintain truly open relationships is a byproduct, a bonus, of vulnerability. Through openness, we are able to let the other person in and let ourselves out. This is an essential requirement for face-to-face synergy. The person whose constant concern is to "cover his tail" simply cannot stay out in front.

Our capacity to interact openly, free of self-defeating defensiveness, increases steadily as we confront stretching objectives, obstacles, difficulties, and possibilities. A crucial requirement in such confrontation is that we must concurrently carry out a quest for new strengths—in ourselves first, and then in others. As individuals, *we are the sum of our strengths*.

As this strong self-awareness builds, we become increasingly able to reach out in a sensitive and truly interested way to others. We begin to develop more capacity to really listen, to really hear, to empathically relate to what the other person is saying and feeling. The tough-minded person learns to relish the growth and stimulation that occurs as a result of such openness.

Positive Listening

We define *negative listening* as "the tendency to hear the other person out and then say what you were going to say anyway." In other words, to listen and not really *hear* at all. Many managers who have absorbed much literature and training in all other facets of communication then negate all that valuable knowledge by this phony practice—purporting to listen when they are only waiting for an opportunity to talk.

Real positive listening must be much more than an act or pose. The tough-minded leader cultivates and develops a genuine desire to know what the team member is *really* saying and feeling. He or she lets the other person *in* and lets himself or herself out. Such enhanced listening and hearing skills are made possible by the kind of emotional vulnerability, confidence, and openness that develop as true strength awareness and orientation evolve. Such confident, positive listening is crucial because in its absence virtually every other so-called technique of excellent leadership will be aborted.

Kinesics

Much has been written about body English, and the general subject is no doubt familiar to all of us. The important thing in face-to-face communication in this connection is that we should not judge the kinesics of another according to past biases or stereotypes. Such stereotypes close us in and close others out—precisely when we should be opening up and stretching for new insights. It is possible to become so preoccupied with the body English of the other person that you introduce phoniness and affectation into the situation.

We must learn, for example, to really reach out to people who present stiff facial expressions, and seek to understand them rather than automatically concluding that they are uninterested or hostile. It could be that they are thinking seriously about what we are saying. Frequently more real communication, the kind that will be retained, is happening in this situation than in the case of the person who seems to respond quickly. When such needless impasses build, it is the major responsibility of the stronger and more mature person to reach out rather than to withdraw. The strong leader reaches out; the lukewarm manager pulls back.

BATTEN'S LAW OF COMMUNICATION

When the communicatee does not understand what the communicator intended, the responsibility remains that of the communicator.

Here is a crucial distinction between the *tough*-minded and the *hard*-minded person. If leaders are confident enough, secure enough, they can reach out and practice an attitude of genuine caring about others. When there is enough of this vital concern and caring, the kinesics will be the right ones.

High Expectations

Perhaps the quickest and most effective way to destroy effective communication is to create a vacuum of recognition, a situation where the other person feels ignored and insignificant. Fundamentally, we all know this, but the failure to act on that knowledge is one of the continuing weaknesses of too many managers.

It is clear that we can denigrate and turn people off by expecting their second best, or their worst. It is equally true (although not attempted as often) that we can create synergistic communication and achievement when we care enough to expect *much*. In this way (and I believe it is the single best way) we help the other person feel significant. To use one's best and most unique gifts and to be able to do so because someone cared enough to discover them is a profound experience. Central to all human needs is this one imperative: to feel in some way significant as a person.

Avoiding Judgments

Face-to-face communication becomes and remains challenging, fresh, and often delightful if we avoid judgments (which are usually based on a preoccupation with the weaknesses of others). Instead of making judgments that close us in and close others out, we should constantly draw on our face-to-face relations, on the liberating power of ongoing dynamic evaluations. We must rigorously resist the temptation to label, box, or categorize others. Such rigid tendencies are not only counterproductive in the managerial sense, but they also take the challenge and joy out of face-to-face relationships. Instead, we should try to see the other person as being in a state of flow, of ongoing growth.

There is a subtle but important difference between judgment and evaluation. Judgment in the usual sense involves looking for and relating to other people's weaknesses. Evaluation stems from a search for and assessment of their values—in short, their strengths.

Reinforcement

Positive reinforcement and our tough-minded term *build on strengths* mean one and the same. One definition of reinforcement is "to strengthen with new force," and it is crucial to perceive that the only way synergistic communication can be built is through the combined strength of the individuals. Weakness is only the absence of a strength. Strong, effective communication cannot be wrought from absences. Each of us is defined or profiled by our strengths. They and they alone comprise what we *are*.

Thus, we must begin looking (and, in fact, never stop looking) for strengths in ourselves. Then, and only then, are we able to perceive, relate to, and further build on the strengths of another person.

Positive reinforcement can be, and often is, only a fatuous phrase unless it derives its nourishment from real self-confidence. And real self-confidence can be fully functional only in relationship to other people. An organization must do all it can to create a work climate in which people are respected for who they are and recognized for their contributions and a job well done.

Caring

We can care enough about other people only if we care about and for the one we see reflected in the mirror. This insight is needed everywhere in the organization, but perhaps especially among human resources executives. In essence, caring is an integral part of face-to-face communication.

We must *care* enough to really *listen positively*. We must care enough to reexamine every policy, program, principle, practice, procedure, and person. Top management is looking for the kind of leader who can make this happen.

Integrity

It means "the state of being entire, wholeness, probity, honesty." Although Webster has not said so, I believe the words *integrity* and *strength* are synonymous. Without one you cannot have a full measure of the other. No material (plastic, wood, iron, paper, or anything else) has strength without integrity of structure.

Please note that none of these single components of good communication will *ensure* excellent communication by itself. Nor will the combination of them all be consistently effective if one ingredient is missing. That ingredient is integrity. It is needed for the crucial melding of all the other elements. It is not only practical and desirable, it is *necessary*. Without integrity there is no credibility, and without credibility, no true communication can happen.

> *To talk much and arrive nowhere is the same as*
> *climbing a tree to catch a fish.*
> —CHINESE PROVERB

COMMUNICATING FROM STRENGTH:
A CASE STUDY IN COMMUNICATION STYLES

Recently, as I was between planes at O'Hare International Airport, I had two very interesting experiences. I was walking along, swinging my briefcase, feeling good, when I heard someone call, "Hey, Joe, how're you doing?"

I turned around and walking toward me was a well-groomed, prosperous-looking man. He held out his hand and said, "Joe, it's good to see you. I think I've read almost every book you've ever written. I think I may have seen all of your films [twenty-one of them]. I've heard a lot of your cassettes and, Joe, awhile back in Harrisburg I heard you speak for three hours."

I was beginning to glow. I said, "It's really good to see you," and started to walk along.

"Wait a minute, Joe," he continued, "I'd like to talk to you a little bit. You know, when you think about it, I've spent literally hours in the dark watching you on film and reading those books. I've spent many hours of reading, I've even listened to your tapes as I lay in bed."

Well, I decided I should spend a little time with this fellow, so I answered, "That's really interesting."

"One of the things that I've gathered from your books is that you be-

lieve in candor. There are three different chapters in your books on candor."

"That's right."

"You reach a lot of people, don't you?"

"Yes, I suppose I do."

"Well, Joe, I'd like to sit down then and talk with you about you. Can we go down to the Red Carpet Room here?"

I had about two hours before my flight, so I agreed. As we walked along, I noticed that this fellow was articulate, intelligent, and sincere. I casually asked, "What did you want to talk about?"

"Joe, like I said, I've really studied you, and I think I have an almost encyclopedic knowledge of your weaknesses."

Startled, I exclaimed, "What?" After a short pause I mumbled, "Gosh, I just realized that I'd better get over to TWA and catch my flight."

"When does your flight leave?" he asked, and, of course, I had to tell him the truth. "No problem," he said, "this'll only take twenty minutes." And so we continued toward the Red Carpet Room.

I found myself walking slightly behind him, hoping I could lose him in the crowd, but he kept an eye on me. When we arrived at the Red Carpet Room, we found an empty corner and sat down for our talk. Sure enough, this was a man of his word; he really had done a job on studying my weaknesses. He proceeded, even though he didn't know he was doing it, to do a job on me. He zeroed right in and, remember, he was articulate, intelligent, and sincere. After about three minutes of this criticism, I felt awful.

I sat there knowing I should be open, that I should hear him because I believe in candor. And yet, in spite of myself, my guard began to go up. The defenses, the retorts, the rebuttal began to form in my mind. I knew I should keep quiet and listen, and so I did—but my defenses had risen very high. Even though I knew I should try to hear every word he was saying, I didn't really hear him at all.

Finally, I sensed that the twenty minutes were about over. By then, I had a little knot in my stomach. Even though I didn't know this fellow very well, I had decided there were a few things I should tell him.

"Yeah, buddy," I said, "and I wanted to mention these things to you—"

At this, he jumped up and held his hand out with a big smile. "It's been great, Joe, I've got to run." And away he went.

I watched him dash out for his plane and muttered after him, "Yeah, buddy, thanks for the dialogue—mostly monologue."

I sat there with all the starch gone from my spine and a knot in my stomach. Finally, I got up and began to walk toward my boarding area. After a bit, I was beginning to feel pretty good again, beginning to get a little bounce back in my stride. As I got within about fifty feet of the boarding area, I heard a voice.

"Hey, Joe, how're you doing?" I turned around and walking toward me was another well-groomed, prosperous-looking guy. He walked up, gave me a warm hand-shake and said, "Joe, it's good to see you."

"Well," I said, somewhat less than honestly, "it's good to see you, too."

"Joe, you won't believe this, but I think I've seen all of your films."

"That's good," I replied, and started to walk on.

"Wait a minute, Joe. Would you believe I've read all your books?" As he continued, I thought to myself, Wow, another one! "And, I've heard a lot of your cassette albums. Joe, you believe in candor, don't you?"

"Well, at the right time and place."

"You reach a lot of people, don't you?"

"Well . . . not as many as you might think."

"I know you do, and you're being modest. Joe, I would like you to walk down to the Ambassador's Lounge with me. I'd like to talk to you for about twenty minutes."

I glanced at my watch and saw that I had about an hour left. "I don't know whether I have time or not."

"What time does your plane leave?" he asked. And, of course, I had to tell him the truth. He smiled and said, "Plenty of time. This will only take twenty minutes."

I started to walk along with him and, as we walked, I noticed four things about this fellow. He was intelligent, articulate, sincere, and he meant well.

I snapped at him, knowing I shouldn't, "What do you want to talk about?"

He smiled again. "Joe, I want to talk to you about your strengths."

Now it was my turn to smile. "Great! Let's talk for a couple of hours."

"I'd like to," he responded, "but I've only got about twenty minutes."

"Then, let's get at it!"

This guy zeroed right in on the strengths he had observed and on the additional strengths he felt I have but haven't even used yet. Even more important, he talked about ways I could use my present strengths better. My defenses dissolved. I let him in and I let me out. The thing called synergy began to happen. If you mix a couple of chemicals together and the result is explosive, it's a synergistic action. When two and two add up to five or more, that's synergy. When the whole is greater than the sum of the parts, that's synergy.

So as we sat there, the combined total of two men was significant. Because I let him in and I let me out, I heard every word he was saying and related to his chemistry. Suddenly I realized with a start that the twenty minutes were over. I wanted to point out some of these good things I ob-

served in him and started to say, "Yes, and I want to say to you—" when he looked at his watch, jumped to his feet, stuck his hand out, and said, "Joe, I've got to run; it's been great to see you." And away he went.

Now, remember, over at the Red Carpet Room, when the first man had to dash for his plane, I said, "Thanks for the dialogue—mostly monologue." Now, to this fellow I used the overused and undercomprehended word communication. *"Thanks, buddy, thanks for the communication."*

Of course by now you have guessed that these two "conversations" are actually composites of hundreds of conversations I have had in dozens of airports over the years. Let's explore some of the key elements involved in real communication. Here are some of the things those "encounters" in O'Hare demonstrate:

- ☐ A discussion of weaknesses usually raises defenses. The only valid reason for identifying weaknesses is to determine what additional strengths are needed or what is needed to further develop existing strengths.
- ☐ When we feel threatened by a weakness-oriented approach, we become defensive whether we really want to or not.
- ☐ Only dialogue and monologue can seep through such defenses. Shared meaning and shared understanding—the essence of communication—can happen only when these defenses are dissolved by a focus on strengths.
- ☐ It is very difficult to be open and vulnerable (necessary conditions for real communication) if approached in a weakness-oriented way.
- ☐ It is relatively easy to begin to dissolve your defenses and really perceive, feel, and hear what the strength-oriented person is attempting to communicate.
- ☐ It is reassuring and reaffirming to learn more about our present and potential strengths. We become able to exchange and share intentions, goals, and expectations.
- ☐ If we dwell on others' weaknesses, we'll never truly get to know one another.
- ☐ If we steadily search for—and *expect to find*—an ever-increasing number of strengths in others, we can come to truly *know* one another.

CHAPTER

THE NEW ENTREPRENEUR

*The wave of the future in American business, it
seems to me, is with the entrepreneurs! The day of
the true entrepreneur seems to have arrived.*
HAROLD GENEEN, FORMER CHAIRMAN AT&T
IN *MANAGING*

The Golden Age of Entrepreneurism may be approaching. Never before
in U.S. history has the awareness of business opportunities been so great.
In "The Spirit of Enterprise" (*Forbes*, February 1987), George Gilder says
of the entrepreneur:

*The entrepreneurs sustain the world. In their career of optimizing cal-
culation . . . they overthrow establishments rather than establish equi-
libria. They are heroes of economic life.*

This new entrepreneur is a synergistic blend of traditional acquisitive, deal-making, self-serving qualities, and the lean, tested, distilled essence of professional leadership principles, seasoned with whiffs of statesmanship.

> *The most valuable one hundred people to bring into*
> *a deteriorating society, like, for instance, Peru,*
> *would not be one hundred chemists or politicians or*
> *professors or engineers, but rather one hundred*
> *entrepreneurs.*
> PSYCHOLOGIST ABRAHAM MASLOW, *EUPSYCHIAN*
> *MANAGEMENT* (1965)

The tough-minded entrepreneur seeks high adventure—all kinds of changes, transitions, and reversals. In this chapter I hope to provide some focus and perspective on the entrepreneurial nation we can become. Much change is imperative!

Ross Perot, the dynamic founder of Electronic Data Systems, has demonstrated with superlative success how this can be done. Always hungry to grow, change, learn, and excel, he recognized over two decades ago that "entrepreneurism" as a hectic, seat-of-the-pants style could not long endure if he was to lead EDS to true global success. He also knew that the tight, tidy, and sterile notion of the professional management process that was then considered the norm—plan, organize, coordinate, execute, and control—was not the full answer. His tough-minded blend of the best of these two possible worlds is now history, and his greatest achievements are almost certainly still to come.

Five remarkable and inspiring examples of the *new* entrepreneur are Steven Jobs of NEXT, Inc. (together with Perot), Mitchell Kapor of Lotus Development Corporation (he recently turned it over to his team), Lane Nemeth of Discovery Toys, Doug Tompkins of Esprit, and Fred Smith of American Express.

ACTION STEPS FOR
ENTREPRENEURIAL SUCCESS

For the past several years my colleagues and I have worked with many small organizations who want to achieve the kind of success that occurred at EDS under the leadership of Perot. In the process we developed some action steps that we recommend to launch successful entrepreneurial rockets. They include:

☐ Establish a company philosophy that reflects your vision of the possible and that stresses integrity, service, quality, constant change, and other tough-minded components of this book. The vision lives in the intensity, focus, and overall example of you, the leader.

☐ Find a market niche, a gap, a unique want, need, or possibility.

☐ Develop a business plan, an action plan—and *get started!*

☐ Incessantly and hungrily seek to learn more and more about the wants and needs of your market. Ask, listen, hear. Survey, research, analyze, and evaluate.

☐ Provide your original investors the opportunity to profit in any feasible and generous way.

☐ Stay organized; use small steps until you have sufficient market, cash flow, teamwork, and knowledge.

☐ Court, woo, and seek to enrich your customers.

☐ Recognize that your people are the be-all and end-all, the alpha and the omega.

☐ Hire the best people you can, using tough-minded methods of strengths discovery, assessment, and deployment.

☐ Provide and lead them through thorough, imaginative, and ongoing training. Train, train, train!

☐ Tie compensation directly to customer-related performance.

☐ Expect their best at all times and reflect that in every dimension of your "P" pyramid.

☐ Give them part of the action and generate entrepreneurial excitement.

☐ Explore the vast untapped possibilities of telemarketing. Imaginatively done, it can be tremendous. Avoid canned approaches. They are a blatant insult to the listener, and they fly directly in the face of the caring, sensitive methods recommended in this book.

☐ Be generous with wages, salaries, profit sharing, benefits, and imaginative new perquisites—and tie them directly to performance. I cannot overemphasize the importance of this.

☐ Develop an error-free system of reporting. Before finalizing your management information system, make the effort to research and determine precisely what kind of information you and your team need, how much you need, and when you need it. Stress *progress* reports, not *activity* reports.

☐ Develop a strategy and specific tactics dedicated to the growth, fulfillment, and profit of your customer. Devote all appropriate training sessions, mentoring sessions, staff meeting agenda, and action plans to this. Make sure that all team members know this is the number-one priority for every job and reward.

☐ Don't neglect pricing policy and strategies. Charge enough to ensure perpetuation of ever-improving quality commitments.

☐ Even as you build a "climate for mistakes" and encourage creativity, innovation, risk taking, and boldness, endeavor to establish a system to *detect* mistakes as early and consistently as possible.

☐ Become obsessed with service, quality, change, and strengths recognition and deployment. Root out passivity. Make room for a passionate style; you will become renewed rather than fatigued.

☐ Make sure that your management controls and checkpoints are fail-safe. Rely on computer applications as *management instruments*, rather than simply data factories. This, I repeat, places the onus on you, the leader. You must determine precisely what *you* need; other needs will then become clear.

☐ If you lose customers, pursue them, woo them, and win them again.

☐ Recognize the paramount and ever-present need for tenacity, resilience, and responsiveness. Anxiety-producing events come with the territory. This is why I continually stress the need for a total lifestyle as a tough-minded leader rather than simply a workweek businessperson. Mental, physical, and spiritual health are crucial to the energetic example required constantly of the passionate leader.

☐ Dare to dream! Envision your company as national or international rather than local or regional. Let your mind soar as you keep both feet on the ground. Help your team members develop excitement, scope, reach, and stretch. Passive puttering has no place in the future for the tough-minded entrepreneur.

☐ Develop and communicate the idea that there are no free lunches. Avoid dependency on government grants, subsidized loans, or "quick fixes." One-minute solutions never work—unless there are a lot of thought, work, and application behind them.

☐ Integrity is the most crucial of all the traits of the tough-minded entrepreneur. That is a given. It allows you to have a less complicated lifestyle and a higher level of mental hygiene—and *it's good business!*

☐ Aim constantly to become the best company in your industry. When Ross Perot founded EDS, it was his consistent and consummate goal from the beginning to become the best technological organization in the world. As EDS began to grow, his team felt the constant lift of this macro-goal. They talked it up. They *felt* it. How *practical* can you get?

☐ Be very careful about diversifying beyond your area of known expertise. While it is important to grow, change, and stretch, it is also prudent to build on known and demonstrated strengths. Diversify into those areas that fit with and supplement your existing business.

☐ Obtain excellent tax and legal counsel, and listen to them.

☐ Do constructive, meaningful, and worthwhile things with the money you earn. Keep your money working at all times.

☐ Sell your business only if and when you are no longer excited and turned on by what you do.

☐   See economic slumps as opportunities for growth. Remember, there's
    always tomorrow.
☐   Come to work each day willing to fail, and never give up—never, never,
    never.

YOUR TOUGH-MINDED BUSINESS PLAN

Strangely enough, many entrepreneurs procrastinate when it comes to
researching and preparing a thorough business plan. Business plans are different for every company, but there are common denominators—tested
guidelines and components; properly developed, they are of inestimable
value. Few legitimate investors will even want to talk to you without one.

Cultivate the habit of constantly asking tough and penetrating questions about you, your market, your team, your goals, your possible pit-
falls—in short, every facet of your existence. Again, it's the tough-minded
dictum:

Ask, listen, hear
in order to determine
wants, needs, and possibilities

This will get you started, by providing both the raw material and the
high-combustion energy you need to begin drafting your business plan. Here
are some key elements to consider in developing this vital management
instrument:

☐   Clear and concise table of contents, a road map for locating specific
    items of information.
☐   Description of your company.
    —What business are you in?
    —What are your principal products, markets, services, and consumer
      applications?
    —What is unique about you and your organization?
    —What is your greatest area of competence?
☐   Marketing and market analysis
    —What is your market?
    —What is happening in your market? What *will* happen?
    —Who are your customers?
    —What are the major mistakes commonly made in your market? What
      are you going to do about them?
    —Have you clearly defined the specificity and possible uniqueness of
      your products or services?
    —Who is your competition?

—Have you talked to and researched prospective customers? What is their reaction?

—Have you determined your marketing strategy? Promotion? Distribution? Pricing? Service? Support? Others?

—Have you defined your *sales* strategy and tactics?

☐ Research and development

—Is you idea patentable or copyrightable? Have you done this?

—Do your plans provide for constant innovation and creativity?

☐ Manufacturing and operations

—What production or operating advantage do you have?

—Do you or will you have a precise knowledge of standard costs for production at various volume levels?

☐ Ownership and management

—What is your need for key people?

—How will you compensate them?

—What knowledge and skills must they have?

—What results have they achieved in your area?

—Do you have a short-range, an intermediate, and a long-range staffing plan?

—Do you have your stock structure? Have you consulted expert legal counsel?

☐ Organization of human resources

—Have you developed a short-range and long-range organizational chart? Job descriptions? Personnel handbook or manual?

—What benefits will you provide?

☐ Money needed and how to use it

—How much money will you need?

—How much are you budgeting for the next three years? Five years?

—Have you prepared a breakeven chart?

—Do you plan to go public? If so, the elements in this brief outline must be thoroughly and thoughtfully fleshed out. If you intend to attract an investment banker, a business plan is not only desirable—it is essential.

☐ Financial information

—Be sure you are working with and paying attention to an excellent accounting firm.

—Ask them to help you develop a financial statement.

The opportunities to start your own business are becoming greater all the time. In summary, clarify and write down your dream. Convert it to specific goals and objectives. Carefully determine all external and internal resources needed. Develop your action plan. And then, *take action!*

Brains and wit will beat capital spending ten times
out of ten.
—ROSS PEROT, FOUNDER, ELECTRONIC DATA SYSTEMS

ARE ENTREPRENEURS DIFFERENT FROM
CORPORATE EXECUTIVES?

Somehow we have developed the idea that entrepreneurs and corporate executives are two different breeds of cat, and never the twain shall meet. In his fine and provocative book, *The Entrepreneur's Guide* (1980), Deaver Brown says:

*Compare for a moment the contrasting temperaments and skills de-
manded by the entrepreneurial and executive careers. One can hardly
imagine more divergent personality profiles. And few successful executives or entrepreneurs seem to vary much from these portraits; so make
sure you select the field most congenial to your personality or you will
suffer untold agonies trying to adopt a foreign identity. For the purposes of your self-analysis, the following pages describe the key entrepreneurial traits in more depth.[1]*

Brown goes on to say that successful entrepreneurial traits include:

Shrewdness   Ability to win confidences of cred-
Boldness   itors and customers
Instinctiveness   Individualism and creativity
Enthusiasm   Ability to resolve a complex assort-
Endurance   ment of problems
Conclusive decision making   Leadership
Tenacity   Product pride
Negotiating skill   Marketing skills
                                  Nerve

And he concludes: "Without a strong dose of these qualities, your venture will flounder like a wounded duck. . . . The new-venture joy will not
be there to bolster you through hard times unless you have a personality
conducive to the task."

These writings merely illustrate two all too common stereotypes:

1. (New York: Macmillan).

☐ The "entrepreneur" is someone who has all the traits listed above, plus a passionate love of business.

☐ The "corporate executive" is essentially custodial, and therefore presumably has none of those traits.

Nothing could be further from the truth. I hope to dispel, even obliterate these stereotypes. In reality, *both* the entrepreneur and the corporate executive must study, master, and exemplify the full transition from managing to leading. Business schools can provide an exciting, productive, and profitable experience when they begin to teach the indivisibility and potential synergy of both worlds as we foster the continued development and emergence of the new leader/entrepreneur.

ENTREPRENEUR'S CREDO

I do not choose to be a common person. It is my right to be uncommon—if I can. I seek opportunity—not security. I do not wish to be a kept citizen, humbled and dulled by having the state look after me.

I want to take the calculated risk, to dream and to build, to fail and to succeed.

I refuse to barter incentive for a dole; I prefer the challenges of life to the guaranteed existence; the thrill of fulfillment to the stale calm of Utopia.

I will not trade my freedom for beneficence nor my dignity for a handout. I will never cower before any master nor bend to any threat.

It is my heritage to stand erect, proud and unafraid; to think and act for myself, to enjoy the benefit of my creations and to face the world boldly and say:

This, with God's help, I have done. All this is what it means to be an entrepreneur.

OFFICIAL CREDO OF AMERICAN ENTREPRENEURS
ASSOCIATION, 1988

John Naisbitt says that in some ways, U.S. entrepreneurs are uniquely qualified to take on the Japanese market. Entrepreneurs simply don't take no for an answer. They also are ready to adapt to market options. And in a country dominated by giants, there is plenty of untapped potential for low-volume custom products. Enough success stories have traveled back to the States to make Japan attractive to a growing number of entrepreneurs who find it makes more sense to compete with Japan on her own turf than to haggle over trade policies at home.

Rather than trying to keep out Japanese chips or raising their prices, American entrepreneurs should be combining foreign memories and other commodity devices with new domestic designs.

The opportunities for bold, resourceful entrepreneurs are going to be breathtaking. To capitalize on these opportunities the new entrepreneur— no less than the new tough-minded executive—will need to understand how to employ positive G forces as never before.

CHAPTER 9

LEADERSHIP AND POWER

Causes, communication, commitment, and courage.
These are the seminal seeds of power.

No matter how accurately the trajectory and orbit of a space vehicle have been plotted, nothing happens unless fuel is in the tank.

Strong, wise, and stretching leadership is simply not possible without *power*—the fuel in the tank. The very nature of the organizational culture, its vision, goals, and specific performance requirements depend utterly on power that is properly developed, deployed, and used.

In his article "Getting Rid of All the Expenses" (*Executive Excellence,* June 1987), Art McNeil says:

Senior managers whose strengths lie in their technical knowledge alone are ill equipped to be active players—let alone winners—in the new arena. Suddenly, just being a "good manager" isn't enough. What's needed are strong leaders who know how to spark energy, enthusiasm, and innovation among the rank and file.

Amazingly few books on management or leadership have dealt with this crucial ingredient. In *Leaders* (1985), Warren Bennis and Bert Nanus discuss the concept of power in relation to a well-known practitioner, Chrysler Corporation's Lee Iacocca:

Almost exclusively because of Iacocca's leadership, by 1983 Chrysler made a profit, boosted employee morale, and helped employees generate a sense of meaning in their work.

He empowered them. In fact, we believe that Iacocca's high visibility symbolizes the missing element in management today (and much of management theory) in that his style of leadership is central to organizational success. Our concept of power and leadership, then, is modeled on the Iacocca phenomenon: power is the basic energy needed to initiate and sustain action or, to put it another way, the capacity to translate intention into reality and sustain it. Leadership is the wise use of this power: Transformative leadership.[1]

But is the example of Iacocca enough for the future? Although his leadership style can be characterized as stimulating and inspirational, I feel Iacocca frequently tends to confuse *directiveness* with *expectiveness*, that is, he tends to *push* rather than to *lead*. Starting with yourself and extending to all the resources in the organization, you should build an approach based on high expectations. Chrysler has certainly begun to do this. (In fact, Chrysler uses the advertising slogan "Expect the Best.") But I see the example of leadership at EDS, under Ross Perot, as more advanced. Perot has demonstrated the power of expective as opposed to directive leadership for twenty years.

In my book *Beyond Management by Objectives* (New York: AMACOM, 1980), I wrote that:

These values and beliefs which comprise the philosophical foundation for the grand design provide the mainstream, the arterial system, of the business. This draws constantly on the vast mental reservoir which holds the combined power of managerial minds in action. Each executive thus finds himself better equipped for policy interpretation and usage which get the job done. To harness and channel this power—to be sure that eight minds add up to more than the sum of their individual potential—is the never-ending challenge of the first-rate chief executive.

1. (New York: Harper & Row, Publishers, Inc.).

Figure 9.1. Upside-down "P" pyramid.

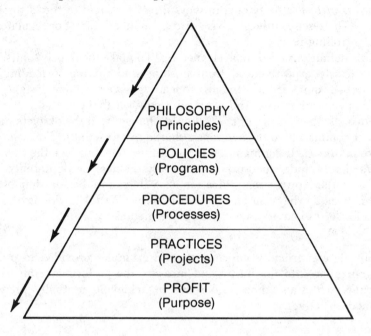

PHILOSOPHY
(Principles)

POLICIES
(Programs)

PROCEDURES
(Processes)

PRACTICES
(Projects)

PROFIT
(Purpose)

In other words, it is necessary to go far beyond the definition of leadership provided by Bennis and Nanus. Leadership must be generated by all the managers, not just by the top executive. And it is up to the top executive to see that this happens, to see that all facets of the organization reflect an expective rather than a directive approach. The very vocabulary of the company, its decision-making processes, and all the actions that impact the bottom line must change.

Let's go back now to the "P" pyramid, which, as we know, reflects the fiber of the entire structure of the organization. I recommend that every dimension, every organic component, of the organization be carefully tooled to reflect these pivotal uses of power. Turn the "P" pyramid upside down (see Figure 9.1) and look at what happens to the flow of power.

NEW DEFINITIONS OF POWER AND CONTROL

The dictionary yields two definitions of power that illustrate the current challenge and the requirements of tomorrow.

1. Great ability to do, act or affect strongly; vigor; force; strength; to be able.
2. The ability to control others; authority; sway; influence.

The first one is for leaders. The second one is obsolete. Incidentally, the word *control* is also defined in ways directly related to the G forces of the past: "To exercise authority over; direct command; direct or regulate; the act of controlling power."

These definitions need to be cleaned up. To make the massive shift from directiveness to expectiveness, from pushing and driving to leading and stretching—in short, from managing to leading—we need new insight, new tools, change, and action. And we need a new vocabulary.

Above all, the concept of *control* must change from the obsolete notion of "direct command" to the awareness shared by the great leaders, the ones who are *pulling* their companies into the future. They believe the best controls are clearly understood expectations, crystal-clear accountability standards, and their own exemplification of values and beliefs that attract followers because they can identify with them. Control in the new tough-minded leadership environment may be defined as:

Control: user-friendly information and examples provided to pull an organization into the future and measure the performance of people, money, materials, time, and space in achieving mutually predetermined objectives.

Thus, the great company of the future will *not* be data-*driven*—it will be data-*responsive*.

A study of winning coaches revealed that they had consistently believed in themselves and in their team, and had high expectations that were clearly communicated.

That's *power!*

THE NEW POWER TOOLS

In *The Change Masters* (1983), Rosabeth Moss Kanter says the three tools of power are information, resources, and support. These tools are certainly useful and germane, and her entire discussion of power is outstanding. I believe, though, that we must go much further in identifying the true power tools for the Age of the Mind.

All intrinsic power is in the mind. All other forms of power are extrinsic.

History has clearly demonstrated the elusive and ephemeral nature of purely directive or coercive power. Military power, economic power, jurisdictional and political power—all become frangible. They can crumble quickly. Mental power alone endures; it demands change, growth, and forward movement.

The power of ideas reflected by example and implemented in a system of clear, focused expectations is the single most crucial and effective form of power for the turbulent decades ahead. Only this type of power can catalyze the dramatic changes needed.

Power Tools for the Age of the Mind

- [ ] Meaningful work for all team members.
- [ ] Tempo—explosive rather than implosive energy.
- [ ] Expectations—results that pull, not push.
- [ ] Accountability—with greatest emphasis on reinforcement and rewards for outstanding performance, with the clear understanding that one does a job or gets out of it.
- [ ] Personal presence—stimulation, emulation, and followership.
- [ ] Ideas—the most practical thing in the world is applied thought, an idea whose time has come.
- [ ] Intuition—decision-making abilities acquired by a process of continuous growth, openness to new experiences, and emotional vulnerability.
- [ ] Granted autonomy, delegation, and empowerment—trust stemming from personal strengths acquisition and deployment.
- [ ] Reports and documents that reflect involvement and commitment of team members.
- [ ] Macro- and micro-optimization through strengths identification and deployment.
- [ ] Stretch and clarity—the true mental power ingredients in all operations.
- [ ] Integrity in action—it builds followership, strengths identification, and focused effort.
- [ ] Esprit de corps—group spirit, sense of pride, and honor shared by those in the same group or undertaking. The belief that "We can do *anything!*"
- [ ] Team synergy—shared meaning, shared values, shared beliefs, shared strengths, shared commitment, shared stretch and reward.
- [ ] Open communication—where strengths and individuality can be optimized and defensiveness minimized.
- [ ] Focus—centeredness; intensity; a laser beam rather than diffused particles.
- [ ] A hunger for learning—so-called leaders who always "know" lose power and credibility; they are obsolete.
- [ ] Unifying lift of transcendent goals, resulting in fused, focused team effort moving forward in concert.

The effect on your team members is powerful indeed. In *Getting the Best Out of Yourself and Others*, Buck Rodgers, former vice-president of marketing at IBM, comments about one dimension:

> *Properly motivated people have a sense of achievement, of being a fundamental part of the total picture. If people feel proud and pleased with their performance, they will then be ready, willing, and able to achieve even more.*[2]

THE POWER OF WORDS

We must change what we *say* because of its certain impact on what we then *do*. My thirty years as a consultant and trainer of managers and leaders have convinced me that we not only become what we think, we become what we say.

Please join my colleagues and me in the cause of completely retooling our lexicon of leadership from the negatively focused vocabulary used in most management contexts.

Some of the worst offenders are:

Drive, driven
Press, pressure
Push, compress, diminish
Tell, direct, order
"I want you . . ." rather than "Will you . . ."
Hard, rigid, static
Get, take
Compel, comply, acquiesce
Invulnerable, defensive
Force, implode, shrink and contract
I, I, I

THE TRUE NATURE OF POWER

Great power should never be vested in those who compulsively seek it. Life is not for pushing, crowding, insisting, driving, coercing, and directing—the stuff of an addictive society.

Rather we are presented with the magnificent expective to *lead*—to pull, stretch, reach, grow, change, confront and, above all, to expect the best. This is the stuff of true leadership. All the truly great leaders of history were masters of the art of clarifying and communicating expectations. The professional exercise of this power is often an awesome responsibility.

2. (New York: Harper & Row, 1987).

John W. Gardner, in his superb book *No Easy Victories*, has some challenging things to say about power and its use.

People who have never exercised power have all kinds of curious ideas about it. The popular notion of leadership is a fantasy of capricious power. The top man presses a button and something remarkable happens. He gives an order as the whim strikes him and the order is obeyed.

The capricious use of power is relatively rare except in some large dictatorships and small family firms. Most leaders are hedged around by constraints—tradition, constitutional limitations, the realities of the external situation, rights and privileges of followers, the requirements of teamwork and, most of all, the inexorable demands of large-scale organization that does not operate on capriciousness. We are immunizing a high proportion of our most gifted young people against any tendencies to leadership. The process is initiated by the society itself. The conditions of life in a modern, complex society are not conducive to the emergence of leaders. The young person today is acutely aware of the fact that he is an anonymous member of a mass society, an individual lost among millions of others. The processes by which leadership is exercised are not exceedingly intricate. Very little in his experience encourages him to think he might someday exercise a role of leadership. This unfocused discouragement is of little consequence compared with the expert dissuasion the young person will encounter if he is sufficiently bright to attend a college or university. In some institutions today the best students are carefully schooled to avoid leadership responsibilities.[3]

What a damning indictment of our society! So much of this vague uneasiness about power is unnecessary. Again, let's tune in on what Dr. Gardner says with such clarity and eloquence:

We don't need leaders to tell us what to do. That's not the American style of leadership in any case. We do need men and women in every community in the land who will accept a special responsibility to advance the public interest, root out corruption, combat injustice and care about the continued vitality of this land. We need such people to help us clarify and divine the choices before us.

We need them to symbolize and voice and confirm the most deeply rooted values of our society. We need them to tell us of our faithfulness or infidelity to those values.

And we need them to rekindle hope. So many of us are defeated

3. The excerpt from *No Easy Victories* is copyright © 1969 by John W. Gardner. Reprinted by permission of Harper & Row, Publishers, Inc.

people—whatever our level of affluence or status—defeated sometimes by life's blows, more often by our own laziness or cynicism or self-indulgence. The first and last task of a leader is to keep hope alive—the hope that we can finally find our way through to a better world—despite the day's action, despite our own inertness and shallowness and wavering resolve.[4]

In my own words:

Again and again the person who fails fails because he is not willing to shoot for the moon, to give his dream all that he has.

Leaders who can accomplish profound changes in our land and in our people must be comfortable and skilled in the use of power—in the deepest, purest sense of the word. And that requires:

Purpose and direction	Dignity
Vulnerability to positive insights	Integrity
Growth	Judgment
Wonder	Wisdom
Caring	Faith
Excellence of example	Love
Excellent work habits	Courage
Inspiration	Hope
Constant credibility	Vision

4. The excerpt from *No Easy Victories* is copyright © 1969 by John W. Gardner. Reprinted by permission of Harper & Row, Publishers, Inc.

## CHAPTER 10

ENHANCING INNOVATION

There is much more opportunity than there are
people to see it.

THOMAS EDISON

"Innovate or die" has become a clarion call in corporate corridors across the land—and high time. The arteries of a corporation harden in direct proportion to the hardening of its management. And rigidity of management stultifies innovative spirits.

INNOVATION STARTS AT THE TOP

In an insightful article, "Managing for Competitiveness" *(Executive Excellence,* February 1988), Guy Hale says the *first* goal of executives seeking to build competitive innovation is an organizational climate that encourages, supports, and rewards innovative effort. Climate *emanates from the very top* (emphasis mine) of the organization, and must be carried out at every level of management.

Take note of the three essentials: *encourage, support,* and *reward.* I'll be talking more about them throughout this chapter.

To provide for innovation, we need a systematic, pervasive climate where the organization's philosophy, principles, policies, procedures, and all the rest of the Ps are ruthlessly renovated. All criteria in the organization should contain intrinsic components of innovation. Recruitment, hiring, selection, and placement procedures must reflect this emphasis. Performance-appraisal criteria and position-evaluation factors must demonstrate this commitment. Compensation, promotions, and perquisites must be directly related.

And finally, those at the top must inspire everyone in the organization with the excitement of the challenge. In organizations committed to innovation, all team members are expected to provide evidence of this commitment by the way they respond, the meetings they schedule, the correspondence, memoranda, reports, and all other feedback mechanisms they're involved in. At 3M more than two hundred products bubble up each year from the research labs that crowd the 435-acre St. Paul campus. Approximately 6,000 scientists and engineers are continuously stirring the pot. It is a *pervasive way of life.*

INNOVATION IN ACTION

Simply talking about innovation is not the answer. Pious statements and catchy slogans are insufficient. A corporate pledge that "we're committed to innovation" must be accompanied by some real planning and follow-through. Figure 10.1 shows a conceptual schema for this kind of plan.

To make the climate of innovation a reality, leaders must be willing to dig in and work. Here are some suggestions.

Schedule Brainstorming Sessions

As a forum for brainstorming, set up "possibility teams." As we'll see in the next chapter, possibility teams use the basics of innovation-stimulating quality circles, but they go much further. Their brainstorming sessions are *led.* There is an all-out search for dormant strengths in every dimension of the organization.

As tough-minded leadership pervades the climate of the organization, there is a keen awareness that the only resources for innovation are the organization's strengths. Thus, the focus of these brainstorming sessions is the search for strengths in the people—how to identify them, how to use them better.

In all ideation sessions, any mention of weaknesses, any use of apostrophe-t's—"didn't," "couldn't," "shouldn't," "can't," "won't," "didn't"—is out of bounds. The *possible* is the focus. Better service and profit through innovation is the ever-present goal.

Figure 10.1. "Cyber" system for innovation.

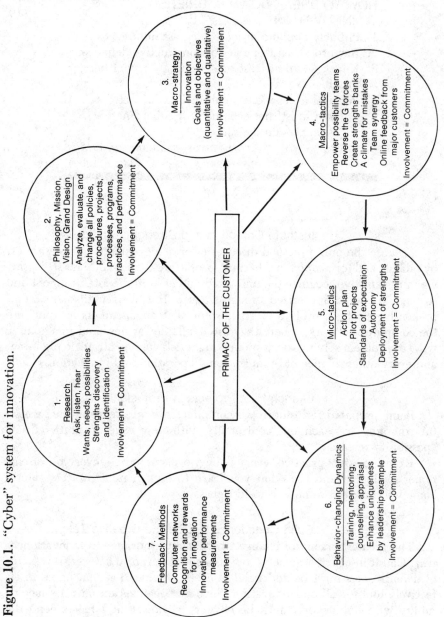

1.
Research
Ask, listen, hear
Wants, needs, possibilities
Strengths discovery
and identification

Involvement = Commitment

2.
Philosophy, Mission,
Vision, Grand Design
Analyze, evaluate, and
change all policies,
procedures, projects,
processes, programs,
practices, and performance

Involvement = Commitment

3.
Macro-strategy
Innovation
Goals and objectives
(quantitative and qualitative)

Involvement = Commitment

4.
Macro-tactics
Empower possibility teams
Reverse the G forces
Create strengths banks
A climate for mistakes
Team synergy
Online feedback from
major customers

Involvement = Commitment

5.
Micro-tactics
Action plan
Pilot projects
Standards of expectation
Autonomy
Deployment of strengths

Involvement = Commitment

6.
Behavior-changing Dynamics
Training, mentoring,
counseling, appraisal
Enhance uniqueness
by leadership example

Involvement = Commitment

7.
Feedback Methods
Computer networks
Recognition and rewards
for innovation
Innovation performance
measurements

Involvement = Commitment

PRIMACY OF THE CUSTOMER

HOW TO BREAK DOWN BARRIERS
TO INNOVATION
1. Publicly applaud at least one past failure.
2. Reward at least one act of constructive defiance.
3. Knock down at least one seemingly trivial barrier
   in a team's way.
4. Perform at least one small facilitating act.
   And insist that each of your subordinate
   managers do the same.

TOM PETERS, *THRIVING ON CHAOS*
(NEW YORK: ALFRED A. KNOPF, 1987)

Institute Computerized Strengths Banks

Because the only practical discoveries or achievements possible are of, by, about, and for *people*, and because people are the sum of their *strengths*, we must quickly recognize the unlimited potential in the establishment and strategic use of computerized strengths banks. In this strengths bank, comprehensive strength profiles or resumes of all team members are put into the computer network, where they are available for new and imaginative ways of problem solving, decision making, crisis coping, strategic planning, and every other nuance of organizational operation and innovation.

Launch Pilot Projects in Profusion

Being prepared for tomorrow's complicated world requires the successful company to reach out continually with new experimentation, new "possibility research."

Examine every practice, every policy, every resource, every bit of customer feedback, and use what you learn to launch pilot projects galore. Some will fail, but some will yield riches.

Build Confidence to Liberate Creative Talent

The greatest enemy of change, the biggest hindrance to innovation, is *fear*. Call it insecurity, anxiety, low concept of self, or whatever, this factor of defensiveness must be addressed in every organization that hopes to effectively tool for all-out innovation. Such an organization must replace timidity with boldness. It must be obvious by now that I recommend the optimization of strengths as the answer. When people know their strengths are recognized and valued, they have the confidence to move away from timidity toward innovation.

All positive innovation stems from the progressive actualization of strengths.

Look for the Simple Answer

One of the enduring roadblocks to quantum leaps in human understanding and synergistic interaction is the persistent belief—widely taught in graduate schools—that complex problems require complex solutions.

We settle for second best, at best, when we settle for a complex answer. The tough-minded leader pulls team members forward in restless search of *simple, tough* answers rather than *complex, easy* answers. Settling for the complex is too easy.

Note, for instance, the team member who responds to your request for a solution with verbosity, oblique sentences, and memos full of compound, complex phraseology. Usually, such complex responses are simply smoke screens for insufficient knowledge. Conversely, the team member who is willing to do the necessary cerebration, dedication, and perspiration can usually present the results succinctly and simply. Complexity is a copout.

Give Generous Recognition and Rewards

The old-style manager who says, "We've got to put a ceiling on this guy—he's making more money than I am," is a symbol of managerial myopia and idiocy. Make sure your innovators, servers, and producers are richly and consistently rewarded from top to bottom and throughout the organization. Take steps to ensure that the number of hours or volume of activity have no relationship to compensation—only performance does. If your performance-based compensation system is right, the more money your team earns, the more you should rejoice.

Encourage Winners

Probably no other company illustrates innovation in action better than the Marriott Corporation. In an interview in *Executive Excellence*, Bill Marriott, Jr., was asked, "Mr. Marriott, what have you learned about how to treat people?" This was his answer:

Motivate them, train them, care about them and make winners out of them. You have to treat people fairly, and you have to treat them as if they're your most important assets, because they are. The competitive edge in this business is people. I'm trying to communicate that I care and that the role they play in the organization is an extremely vital one. I'm trying to drive out fear. No manager can be fired unless he or she has been warned in writing three times. In performance reviews we

applaud strengths, pinpoint areas that need improvement and deter-
mine what assistance is needed.[1]

Create a Climate for Mistakes

When *Tough-Minded Management* was published in 1963, one of its
most controversial topics was the idea of deliberately seeking the kind of
boldness and riskiness that would yield mistakes. I recommended specifically that mistakes be encouraged in a calculated effort to stimulate innovation and creativity. It is somewhat amusing now to recall the furor this
created.

With tongue in cheek, I often ask seminar audiences to finish this sen-
tence: "Anything worth doing is worth doing. . . ." Of course they always
answer "right" or "well." I then recommend that if they *really believe* that
is true, they should tell little children *not* to do it again when they fall
down or mispronounce a word. The hesitancy and downright fear engen-
dered by that familiar aphorism cause incalculable losses in innovation,
productivity, and happiness at all ages and levels. We see its insidious impact on all the Ps in many organizations.

> *People who take risks are the people you'll lose*
> *against.*
> JOHN SCULLEY, CEO, APPLE COMPUTERS

Build words like *boldness, risk, energy,* and *calculated vulnerability*
into the entire infrastructure of your organization.

Do you have the courage to fail your way to success?

Obtain Online Feedback From Major Customers

Do you want to go well beyond simply giving lip service to the primacy
of the customer? Then seriously explore the feasibility of setting up an online computer network that permits your major customers to transmit their
wants, needs, problems, and possibilities directly to a designated coordination center in your company. And then listen, listen, listen to the people
who buy. Rank Zerox Ltd. has informed 130 of its European executives
that salary increases will be based *exclusively on customer satisfaction,* as
measured by an independent survey of client attitudes and an internal audit
of repeat sales. Few companies give the customer so loud a voice in compensation decisions—but they should!

1. "Ten Million Chances to Excel Each Day," April 1986. Used by permission
of J. W. Marriott, Jr.

HOW TO SQUELCH INNOVATION

Innovation cannot flourish and endure in a driven, directive, tight, screwed-down climate. Here are some negative ways to ensure that you'll evolve into or remain a sterile, drifting, noninnovative organization:

1. Be defensive and cautious at all times.
2. Require documentation and proof of everything proposed.
3. Require total compliance and conformance from your team.
4. React to symptoms rather than seeking causes.
5. Be preoccupied with weaknesses and apostrophe-t's.
6. Base compensation on seniority, activity, education, color, race, and personal flattery.
7. Look out for number one—yourself—at all times.
8. Let people know what you're against.
9. Engage in negative listening. Hear them out and then say what you were going to say anyway.
10. Withhold praise at all times.
11. Make sure your people know you are a "knower" rather than a "learner."
12. Encourage your people to compete *with each other* rather than with their own self-generated goals.
13. Require rigid compliance with all forms of organizational protocol.
14. Go by the book.

Don't give in to these negatives. Seek instead to stimulate innovation wherever possible.

CHAPTER **11**

NUTS AND BOLTS OF
INNOVATION AND PRODUCTIVITY

Whether called "task forces," "quality circles,"
"problem-solving groups" or "shared-responsibility
teams," such vehicles for greater participation at all
levels are an important part of an innovating
company.
ROSABETH MOSS KANTER
THE CHANGE MASTERS

This chapter is designed to provide perspective and focus on the crucial steps needed for American businesses to remain viable and prosper in the turbulent decade ahead. Using a thorough and comprehensive understanding of these vital steps and processes, we move toward the understanding and application of a total productivity system—the positive G climate—which takes the progressive organization of the 1990s into, through, and beyond typical "quality circles" to the more advanced "possibility teams."

Figure 11.1. Tough-minded quality circles: Basic sequence and procedure.

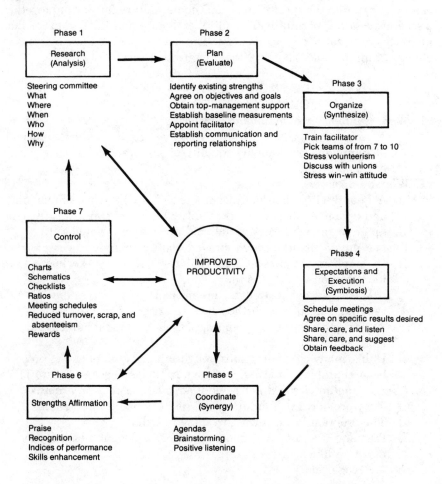

QUALITY CIRCLES FOR AMERICA

Quality circles are a viable tool if used properly. In fact, a number of U.S. companies have long known and taught, in piecemeal fashion, the techniques implicit in the typical approach to quality circles. We simply haven't done a sufficient job of organizing, systematizing, and implementing these techniques.

The tough-minded quality circle (Figure 11.1) is for the company wanting to move beyond the typical quality-circle thinking of the past, but not quite ready yet for the additional expective sophistications of possibility teams. While this entire book is, in a very real sense, about teams and team building, here I am discussing an approach that is designed to yield much more than a fine team functioning *within* an organizational unit. In this chapter I describe the specific steps and nomenclature for putting together a synergistic *system* of multilevel, multidisciplinary, multifaceted teams that are truly organizationally ecumenical. The sole purpose of these teams is to change, improve, and challenge the organization as a whole.

COMMON QUESTIONS ABOUT
QUALITY CIRCLES

1. *What is a tough-minded quality circle?*
   - ☐ A group of seven to ten people who meet regularly for the purpose of improving productivity, quality of performance, morale, product, and profit.
2. *Who are members?*
   - ☐ A quality circle is usually composed of people from similar units and organizational levels. (Possibility teams, in contrast, are made up of people who work at any and every appropriate level.)
3. *What is unique about a tough-minded quality circle?*
   - ☐ Its emphasis on present and potential strengths. Weaknesses are identified only to determine:
     —What additional strengths are needed
     —What is needed to further develop existing strengths
   - ☐ An expective vocabulary and approach are taught rather than directive ones.
   - ☐ Unlike many circle programs, tough-minded quality circles proceed beyond problem analysis, as shown in the sequence in Figure 11.2.
4. *How do quality circles differ from other improvement programs?*
   - ☐ They provide much interpersonal discussion and interaction.
   - ☐ The program has its own governing board.
   - ☐ Presentations to management provide an excellent means for members to fulfill their needs for:
     —Recognition
     —Security
     —Opportunity
     —Belonging
   - ☐ Facilitators and members are familiar with tough-minded, expective dynamics.
   - ☐ Membership is voluntary.
   - ☐ Participants are paid for the time they spend in circle meetings.
5. *What results should be expected from quality circles?*
   - ☐ Increased feelings of participation and identification with company and unit goals.
   - ☐ Increased quality output from equipment, procedures, processes, and people.

Figure 11.2. Proposal process sequence.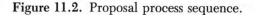

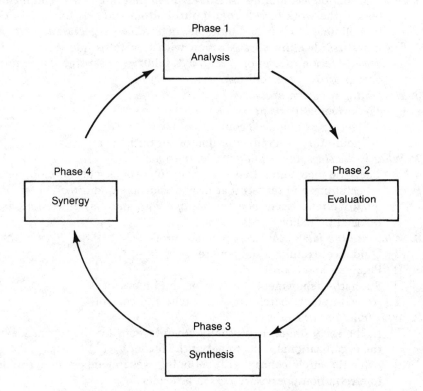

- [ ] Greater cooperation, safety, and pride.
- [ ] Reduced turnover and absenteeism.
- [ ] Reduction in scrap and waste.
- [ ] Greater effectiveness of peer influence to meet stretching standards.
- [ ] Increased feelings of positiveness and demonstrated creativity.
- [ ] The feeling on the part of team members that they are truly treated as contributing resources, as valued people.
- [ ] Reduced errors.
- [ ] Insight into effective teamwork.
- [ ] Greater feelings of involvement.
- [ ] The formation of a preventive rather than crisis-coping attitude.
- [ ] Fewer accidents.
- [ ] Better internal communications.
- [ ] Better relationships, greater openness and trust, between team members and leaders.

- [ ] Increased personal and leadership qualities.
- [ ] The confidence, morale, and motivation that builds when all members of the work force, from top to bottom and side to side, work in a climate of clear and mutually determined expectations.
- [ ] A restless, healthy *un*satisfaction with the status quo (remember, *dis*satisfaction focuses on yesterday's failures; *un*satisfaction focuses on tomorrow's possibilities).

6. *How is the program organized?*
   - [ ] The principal parts are:
     —Steering or guidance committee
     —Facilitator, program coordinator, or optimizer

7. *What is the steering or guidance committee?*
   - [ ] The guidance committee is a group of people who develop clear expectations and targets that provide purpose and direction for the quality circle. Each member has one vote and major decisions are reached by ballot or consensus.

8. *What are the facilitator's responsibilities?*
   - [ ] Guidance, training, and counsel
   - [ ] Planning and coordination
   - [ ] Strengths deployment, facilitation, and focus
   - [ ] Agreed-upon research, measurement, and control

9. *Who functions as leader?*
   - [ ] In the early stages, it is usually advantageous for the supervisor of the organizational units to act as the leader.
   - [ ] After the circle concept is functioning well, members may decide to elect a nonsupervisory person as leader.

10. *How does the circle operate?*
    - [ ] The major elements of the process are:
      —Problem identification
      —Problem selection
      —Problem analysis
      —Recommendations to management
    - [ ] Recommendations to management are carefully and thoroughly planned to reflect completed staff work, which will stress possibilities for:
      —Increased productivity
      —Increased morale
      —Increased quality
      —Increased profit
      —Increased effectiveness and efficiency
      —Increased innovation and calibrated change
    - [ ] Presentation of recommendations to management may also be attended by the members of the steering committee, the facilitator,

and other managers and experts as appropriate. It is truly a high-light of the entire program and should be planned and executed with great care.

11. *What occurs at a circle meeting?*
    □ Identifying and agreeing on the specific objectives for the meeting.
    □ Further development, training, and insights of members.
    □ Asking, listening, and hearing to determine wants, needs, and pos-sibilities—listen, listen, listen, to the people who do the work!
    □ Agreement on sequence of actions to be taken.
    □ Formulating actual action plans, timetables, and controls.

12. *When and where are meetings held?*
    □ This will vary widely. Some rules of thumb are:
    —An hour once a week, or whatever is agreed upon
    —During working hours, if practical and appropriate
    —In a facility where interruptions are minimal

13. *What training is needed?*
    □ The facilitator is trained by appropriate experts or consultants.
    □ Leaders are trained by the facilitator with guidance from the con-sultant.
    □ Circle members will be trained by the leaders with help from the facilitator and consultant as needed.

An organization productivity climate, which was shown schematically in Figure 5.2, "A system of leadership by expectations," is a key element to assure the success of quality circles.

KEYS TO SUCCESS WITH QUALITY CIRCLES

The mechanics of quality circles are basically simple but, paradoxically, highly variable from one organization to another. In this brief overview, I hope to provide some tested common denominators that enhance innovation and productivity.

1. Participants should share a mutual understanding of the vision, mission, and objectives of the organization as a whole and of their organiza-tional unit.

2. They should be encouraged and stimulated to be:
    a. Creative and innovative, with a wide variety of talents, styles, in-terests, and aptitudes
    b. Willing to rock the boat
    c. Restless and *un*satisfied
    d. Candid, vulnerable, and open
    e. Curious and questing

     f. Committed to identifying current and potential strengths in all areas
       of the company

     g. Committed to values, goals, and levels of excellence bigger than self

3. Communication processes, both intergroup and intragroup, should be characterized by expective and nondirective language rather than arbitrary or directive language. Decision making should be relatively decentralized. Enhancement of the dignity of the individual must always be the highest priority.

4. Rewards for innovative contribution must be clearly perceived, felt, and understood. All ambiguity must be eliminated so that the relationship of productive performance to rewards is crystal clear.

5. Management must be willing to provide much more information than is typically shared.

6. All participants should clearly perceive where their role and contributions fit into and affect the overall scheme of operations.

7. Management's actions must pervasively illustrate asking, listening, hearing.

8. Training and education must be recognized as an ongoing, never-completed process. Instructors and facilitators should be thoroughly educated in holistic understanding, insights, and applications.

All these steps together illustrate the sequence and forging of an "Expective Leadership System" (ELS). You have already seen one overall schema of such a system, the cybernetic circle in Figure 5.1. Such a system is, of course, flexible and should be adapted to the needs of individual organizations.

MORE ANSWERS

Konosuke Matsushita, head of Matsushita Industries and an acknowledged leader in the areas of Japanese productivity and innovation, played a large role in the evolvement of quality circles. In the early 1960s, when he asked me for permission to use my cybernetic circle of quality, he was reacting to the circle and first tier at the center of Figure 2.1, the cybernetic circle of becoming. Refer back to the figure. The two additional tiers (actually the components of possibility teams) were developed by my company in the years that followed.

In the complete, fully functioning organization of the future, planned skillful *involvement* is essential and lends itself to *commitment* when executed with *conviction.* Regrettably, in most instances the potential payload of this approach is missed because its cybernetic possibilities are not sufficiently understood and practiced.

What, then, does the three-tiered amalgam in Figure 2.1 imply? In order to explore and understand how and why we can truly define and move *beyond* quality circles, we need to understand something that Japanese businesspeople already seem to know—that is, that the *art* of professional leadership is composed of two aggregates or components:

Mechanics + Dynamics = Complete Leadership

These components must not be considered as discrete, mutually exclusive elements, but rather as key elements that cannot be divided.

Let's examine this total cybernetic system. Visualize the three processes in the smallest tier as the overall organizational method of operation to be desired: again, involvement must precede commitment if it is to be executed with conviction. The product of such involvement, commitment, and conviction is constantly applied to the ever-improving, ongoing, updating, perpetuating use of the "P" pyramid of the organization. A close parallel exists between the seven Ps of this pyramid and the seven Ss in Richard T. Pascale and Anthony G. Athos's book, *The Art of Japanese Management.*[1] These Ss refer to strategy, structure, systems, style, skills, staff, and shared values.

Visualize further that this process is fueled and vitalized by the ten elements on the next tier. This tier represents a mix of both mechanics and human dynamics. For instance, consider the *mechanics* involved in creating and installing administrative procedures to ensure that jobs are evaluated, salary grades created, and salary ranges constructed on the basis of performance. The actual employee performance, however, is strongly conditioned by the *dynamics* of training and development programs that teach, sharpen, and reinforce such values as caring, listening, and examining and identifying strengths.

On the third tier, you perceive again the mechanics—goals, action plans, performance standards, and timetables. These are vital—but not necessarily unique—to any well-led and well-managed organization. The uniqueness begins to form, synergize, and move beyond quality circles to a total cybernetic system when we integrate and blend the *dynamics* (items 7 through 16 of the third tier) with the *mechanics*.

At the heart of this entire cybernetic process, we perceive the central, pervasive need for education and counsel fed by a vision of potential and possibilities.

MOVING TO THE NEXT LEVEL:
POSSIBILITY TEAMS

The quality, cadence, and tempo of our lives derive directly from the quality of our expectations. The quality, cadence, and tempo of our organizational innovation and productivity also derive directly from the quality

1. (New York: Warner Books, 1982).

of these expectations. The preliminary mechanics of possibility teams are almost exactly like those of tough-minded quality circles. The significant difference is the stress placed on moving beyond analysis to synergy, and plugging in the full vitality of the tough-minded expective leadership system.

The conceptual foundation for possibility teams is built on four key premises.

1. *Significance*—the deepest and most consistent of human needs, both on and off the job. The need to feel significant as a person is best met when team members can understand and experience:
    a. Clear and meaningful expectations—the finest gift one person can give another
    b. A growing understanding of current and potential strengths
    c. Involvement in formulating the commitments they are expected to fulfill
2. *Quality of work*—and concomitant productivity—is greatly enhanced when significance, clear expectations, strengths enhancement, and involvement are clearly and skillfully integrated into the company's "P" pyramid.
3. The unending challenge is to search for, identify, stimulate, and build on the *strengths of all resources* in the organization. This will positively affect the quality of work life, and therefore innovation and productivity, in the most direct way possible.
4. *The logical deployment of strengths* determines the answers to familiar questions of span of control, unity of command, and logical assignment. The fusion of strengths to achieve objectives is, in the final analysis, what organization is all about. From this perspective, the pragmatic questions become:

    What is controlled?
    What should function with unity?
    What should be logically assigned (deployed)?

And in every case the answer revolves around identified strengths.

Next, we see a conceptual schematic for creating possibility teams (Figure 11.2). This figure is designed to illustrate the internal process carried out in preparation for submitting the completed proposal to the appropriate level of management.

In Figure 11.3, we see what can be a useful planning guide and instrument for the possibility team. This can be particularly useful as an aid in phase 1 of Figure 11.1. Figure 11.3 denotes optimum factors in possibility

Figure 11.3. Beyond the quality circle.

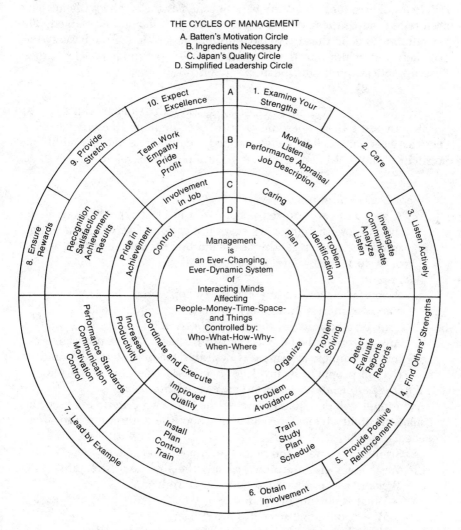

THE CYCLES OF MANAGEMENT
A. Batten's Motivation Circle
B. Ingredients Necessary
C. Japan's Quality Circle
D. Simplified Leadership Circle

teams. After the possibility team has targeted an area in which to actualize possibilities, an imaginative expansion and application of Figure 11.3 can be useful.

You will notice that these same ideas also underlie tough-minded quality circles. These ideas, and the basic mechanics that embody them, have been tested, authenticated, and proved, and they should be retained. The key differences lie in the effective day-to-day integration of the basic system of beliefs and values into the organization's "P" pyramid: policies, procedures, practices, programs, purpose.

Common Questions About Possibility Teams

In answering these questions, I will try to highlight the crucial differences between an excellent tough-minded quality circle and the additional possibilities (no pun intended) inherent in a possibility team.

1. *What is a possibility team?*
   - ☐ A group of seven to ten people who meet at regular intervals for the purpose of improving every dimension of service, innovation, spirit, fused focus, and vision—and therefore productivity, quality of performance, morale, product, and profit.
2. *Who are members?*
   - ☐ People who work at any and every appropriate level, who have a common interest in, and commitment to, improvement.
3. *Who can be a member of the possibility team?*
   - ☐ Any person on the payroll can join the team. As the program grows into a complete system, it is desirable for a great number and variety of people to be involved. Symbiotic synergism is the goal.
4. *What is unique about tough-minded possibility teams?*
   As in tough-minded quality circles, the following criteria are used, but since possibility teams are wider in scope, the criteria are also broadened:
   - ☐ Strengths, current and potential, are emphasized.
   - ☐ Weaknesses are interpreted as only the absence of strengths.
   - ☐ Weaknesses are identified only to determine:
     —What is missing or lacking
     —What additional strengths are needed
     —What is needed to further develop existing strengths
   - ☐ Positive G force vocabulary and approach are taught and used, rather than a directive or negative G force.
   - ☐ Functional analysis, evaluation, synthesis, and synergy of macro as well as micro organizational units, are taught and applied in depth. These four steps are shown in Figure 11.2.
5. *What results do possibility teams produce?*
   Expect all the results shown for tough-minded quality circles, *plus* the following:

- ☐ Greater empowerment and renewal of people
- ☐ Greater enhancement of individuality
- ☐ More pervasive organizational impact
- ☐ Better leadership development
- ☐ A more complete reversal of the G forces
- ☐ Improved team spirit and teamwork
- ☐ Increased return on investment (average ratio of six to one)
- ☐ Improvement in interdepartmental communication and cooperation
- ☐ Constant focus on and guidance from the vision and mission of the organization
- ☐ The constant discovery of new possibilities fed and fueled by the corporate dream

6. *Specifically, in what ways do possibility teams go beyond quality circles?*
- ☐ All recommendations are fueled by and keyed to the basic philosophy of the organization.
- ☐ There is a high degree of interpersonal discussion and interaction.
- ☐ The program has its own built-in leadership.
- ☐ Whereas some team members feel that the term *quality circle* sounds impersonal, coercive, and remote, the very nature of the term *possibility team* is inspiring.
- ☐ The presentations to management reflect a higher level of completed staff work and provide an excellent means for members to fulfill their needs for:
  —Recognition
  —Security
  —Opportunity
  —Belonging
  All of which add to the most important of all: significance.
- ☐ Facilitators and members have been thoroughly trained in tough-minded expective dynamics.
- ☐ Membership is voluntary.
- ☐ Participants are paid for the time they spend in team meetings.
- ☐ Possibilities for new and better ways are considered to be implicit in every aspect and dimension of the organization.

This total systems approach to enhancing a positive G-force climate with possibility teams creates virtually unlimited possibilities. It is based totally on positives, on strengths, on the tested and crucial principle that meaningful involvement stacks the deck in favor of commitment carried out with conviction. This was the key tough-minded paradigm grasped by Konosuke Matsushita.

Suggested Implementation Timetable

1. For possibility teams to succeed, management support at the top levels of the organization is crucial. Senior managers must make a commitment to encourage and reinforce creative idea development and implementation from employees at grass-roots levels of the organization. If there is some question about adequate support, a management climate survey is recommended.
2. Make the decision to implement possibility teams.
3. Appoint a guidance committee (if you decide to have one).
4. The trainer, or other appointed individual, learns the principles for possibility teams and techniques for training others in the process.
5. Guidance committee members are trained in the possibility team process.
6. Departments and other work units are asked to volunteer to be part of the possibility team program.
7. Three work areas are selected for the initial phase of implementation from among those volunteering.
8. Volunteers for team membership are solicited from each of the three areas selected.
9. Seven to ten members, along with their immediate supervisor, are chosen from each area.
10. The team members and their supervisor (who will be the team leader) are trained by the trainer in the possibility team process.
11. Those three areas implement possibility teams, with the trainer available to assist with any problems that may be encountered.
12. Additional teams are trained and implemented on a schedule that allows for smooth implementation and adequate trainer time.
13. Assign a time interval for each key step.

Important Management Information
for Possibility Teams

With possibility teams, your focus should be on the stretch, growth, and development of team members. As the team members respond, the company will benefit in many ways: increased employee productivity and job satisfaction; reduced turnover rates and absenteeism; improved cost effectiveness. It is critical, however, that these results be viewed as *bonuses* only. As targeted goals, they will not be attainable. Employee growth and development must be emphasized.

Make a commitment to ongoing employee growth that extends far beyond the initial possibility team's training. This commitment includes sharing information about company operation, accounting and manufacturing principles, public relations, insurance considerations, marketing research, mission, dreams, and goals, so that team members understand company operations. Advanced training modules are also important in developing team skills.

Be certain that you actively listen to the ideas and recommendations of team members by sincerely praising team accomplishments and implementing at least half of the team recommendations. Be careful to avoid controlling or even influencing possibility team topics; this helps avoid the impression that possibility teams are a management tool or trick. Provide adequate time during working hours for team activities, and provide the information and resources the teams request. Recognize that possibility teams will help their organization attain new heights and success levels—and that they can expect the best!

CHAPTER **12**

BUILD AND MOTIVATE
YOUR TEAM

*To build a winning team, you must first of all
develop a winning attitude.*
LOU HOLTZ
HEAD FOOTBALL COACH, NOTRE DAME

Primary among the qualities that lift great leaders above second-raters
and also-rans is commitment to building a team—a team with transcendent
focus, unity, loyalty, shared-strengths emphasis, and a high level of committed energy. Much has been written and said in recent years about team
building, and many esoteric devices have been proffered. I believe, though,
that the first step in the team-building process is to determine the fundamental qualities, the attitudes, that leaders for the year 2000 should have.

106

ATTITUDE IS EVERYTHING

Ten tough-minded attitudes characterize great leaders and team builders. These qualities remain the same, no matter what area of business, no matter what time period. They are:

1. *Expect the Best.* Believe that there are strengths, possibilities, and latent richness in all situations, people, and events.
2. *Develop an Action Plan.* Each week, target all key wants and needs in advance, and list priorities under each. Then make sure you accomplish all *needed* actions before you undertake any *wanted* actions. You'll get more done, and you'll also enjoy your wants more when you do get to them.
3. *Share, care, and dare to be aware.* Cultivate a curious and zestful interest in the uniqueness of your team members. Ask—and really *listen.* Focus on their strengths, to defuse, diffuse, and dissolve their defenses. Help them feel good about you and your vision, mission, and goals. Provide assurance and *re*assurance, affirmation and *re*affirmation, by what you think, say, and are.
4. *Think through and write down your dream.* If you don't have a dream, how will you make a dream come true? Once you have sculpted a dream—a stretching and transcendent expectation—it then becomes possible to develop specific goals, objectives, action plans, and timetables that are fueled and guided by that dream. You may find it hard work, but the rewards are well worth it.
5. *Prospect for gold.* The average "good" leader perceives "good" potential in each team member. Excellent executives, the leadership artists, constantly look for and expect to find new strengths in their team members. In short, the great leaders incessantly seek to mine new human riches, new possibilities. They help their team members visualize possibilities, benefits, and applications that they would never think of otherwise. Their every action enhances rather than diminishes all with whom they have contact.
6. *Incessantly seek knowledge and growth.* Master and polish your knowledge of the features, benefits, and uniqueness of your product or service. Visualize your customers *and* team members as walking bundles of strengths and possibilities. Commit to better relationships with these people by learning more about their strengths, dreams, and motives.
7. *Provide unusual and unparalleled service.* It is no coincidence that the second of the three basic beliefs of IBM reads: "We want to give the best customer service of any company in the world." Champions outserve all competitors.
8. *Believe in the magic of believing.* Great leaders, those who are real pros and artists, believe deeply and unceasingly that the hoped-for thing is

fact. This conditions the mind, body, and spirit—and the results. It *becomes* fact! Thomas Watson, Jr., former CEO of IBM, says, "We constantly acted as though we were much bigger, much more sophisticated, much more successful than any balance sheet might bear out." IBM truly illustrates "the magic of believing."[1]

9. *Radiate energy, joy, and upness.* Continuously and incessantly search for new strengths in *you*. Recognize that a weakness is only an indication of a missing or insufficiently developed strength. Then you'll find it much easier and more invigorating to look for and relate to the strengths of your customers and your team. Develop your own strengths notebook and write down every strength you can think of. Then add one additional strength each week for a year. Many successful executives continue this process year after year. It stimulates amazing growth and change. It builds confidence, purpose, and direction, and an ever-growing awareness of what *fuels* them.

10. *Harness the power of love.* An out-glowing of care, service, and commitment to the customer's desires is a common denominator in the tool kit of the persuasive leadership artist. *Love is the toughest-minded emotion in the world* and the finest mental and spiritual nutrient you can possess for a total life of fulfillment and actualization. It is truly the nutrient that grows winners.

PRACTICAL TIPS FOR TEAM BUILDERS

These techniques will help you forge a superb team by optimizing the useful.

- ☐ Delegate in terms of *results expected.*
- ☐ Make sure you are doing the right thing before concentrating on doing the thing right.
- ☐ When developing performance standards, take the time to guarantee the team member understands the what, where, when, who, how, and why. Ask for feedback to ensure this.
- ☐ Make sure that team members understand precisely how much authority they have to accomplish agreed-upon standards or results commitment.
- ☐ If the job or assignment is not clearly understood, be sure you realize that three fingers are pointing back at you every time you point to a fault or dwell on a weakness.
- ☐ Make sure the method of reporting back to you is clearly understood.

1. *A Business and Its Beliefs: The Ideas That Helped Build IBM* (Ann Arbor, Mich.: UMI).

☐ Let team members—and expect them to—make their own decisions whenever feasible and practical.

☐ When you promote a person, do not be overly influenced by technical skills. Recognize that interpersonal or "people" skills are what get results.

☐ Recognize that every supervisor is a coach, a trainer, a leader, an inspector, sometimes an inventor, and always an expector.

☐ Remember that a fine example is worth ten thousand words.

☐ Be sure your people know:
—Rules and regulations—safety, conduct, etc.
—Quotas, schedules, and shipping dates
—Appropriate methods, procedures, and processes
—Personnel policies and benefits

☐ Make sure that deviations from agreed-upon expectations are dealt with when they happen. Also that superior performance is recognized immediately.

☐ Problems of attendance, punctuality, and accidents should be dealt with immediately, not deferred.

☐ Try to ensure that *all* your people are growing in some way.

☐ Control your emotions. Leaders who blow hot and cold keep people feeling insecure and relatively unproductive.

☐ Take care of the company, and it will take care of you.

☐ Try to make sure your people would say of you: "I always know what is expected, and you take the time to explain why."

☐ Vary your reading and experiences so that you are constantly becoming broader and more informed about other facets of your company and the world around you.

☐ Try to become known by your fellow leaders as an unusually cooperative and supportive person.

☐ Strive to always think before you act, then be decisive, follow through, and expect commitment and results.

☐ Be a concerned leader rather than a worried one.

☐ Recognize that, with skill and effort, you can help increase your people's *hope* in every performance appraisal and in all kinds of face-to-face situations.

☐ Never overlook a valid opportunity to reinforce or build people in the eyes of their peers.

☐ Flexibility, Imagination, Resourcefulness, and Enthusiasm add up to FIRE. Put some fire into yourself, your people, and your job.

☐ Believe that all team members can be creative—and *expect* them to be.

☐ Learn to listen with both your mind and heart. Really *hear* what people say.

☐ Shun defensiveness. Defensive people and actions only shrink and go backward.

☐ Make your schedules realistic. Develop deadlines only after you have carefully considered all the potential problems in the people, money, material, time, and space for which you are accountable.

☐ Gossip and innuendo have no place in the top-notch department. Make sure your example and expectations reflect this.

☐ Strive constantly to become a skillful questioner. Learn to probe, analyze, and examine before forming a conclusion.

☐ Say nothing about people that you would not tell them personally.

☐ Study report writing. Learn to present performance data with clarity, brevity, and validity.

☐ Organize yourself so that time becomes an asset, not a liability. For instance, make weekly and daily lists of your most important musts and wants, then do all your musts before starting on your wants.

☐ Improve your speaking skills. Practice with a tape recorder and a mirror until you like the way you sound. Work on pace, relaxation, and warmth.

☐ Know the difference between delegation and abdication. *Delegation* means to assign, trust, instruct. If needed, provide for orderly and mutually agreed-upon feedback with the full realization that you are still accountable for seeing that team members understand and fulfill their responsibility, authority, and accountability. *Abdication* means to relinquish all control and followthrough, and hope the assignment gets done somehow.

☐ Stay healthy and fit. There is nothing more practical than to have your body and mind functioning as well as circumstances permit. You are able to think better, make better decisions, and lead better.

☐ Expect to succeed. Expect excellence from yourself and your colleagues.

☐ Know the difference between the conversational styles of the expective and directive leader. Expective leadership says:

Will you do . . . ?
What do you think . . . ?
Can you get this done by . . . ?

Directive leadership says:

I want you to . . .
Don't you think . . . ?
Can't you get this done by . . . ?
Get this done by . . .

Try to eliminate *all* apostrophe–t's from your vocabulary.

☐ Develop the habit of looking at a workload, procedure, program, process, or unit of people that need improvement and following this sequence:

Eliminate, Combine, Rearrange, Simplify
or
Analyze, Evaluate, Synthesize, Synergize

☐ Organize meetings this way:
—Carefully prepare your agenda.
—Encourage the ideas and critiques of all. Draw them out. Ask, listen, and really *hear*.
—Make sure all members know the objective of the meeting.
—Request feedback to ensure understanding.
—Conclude the meeting with a summation of the accomplishments and courses of action agreed upon.
—Thank the group members for their participation and cooperation.

☐ Visualize yourself as a leader, not a pusher. Leaders request and expect. Pushers order, demand, and push. Leaders know what they are *for*. Pushers know what they are *against*. Leaders are emotionally vulnerable. Pushers are defensive.

☐ Skill and firmness in asking will virtually always accomplish more than ordering.

☐ Condition all working relationships and decisions with the belief that people should *not* be evaluated on the basis of color, creed, sex, seniority, or religion. Rather, they should always be evaluated in terms of accomplishment and performance.

☐ Carefully study all descriptive traits in the next chapter, "Leadership in the Twenty-First Century."

☐ To cope with unsatisfactory team members:
—Avoid hiring a potential problem. Screen very carefully.
—Stay in close touch with your team so that potential problems can be discovered early and dealt with.
—Make sure they know precisely what the job expectations are.
—Make sure they have all the materials, tools, and coaching they might need.
—Make sure *your* example is what it should be.
—Be candid, be specific, build on strengths, listen, and hear.
—Assume the team member is right until proven wrong.
—Get to know team members as well as you can. Attempt to help them see and feel a relationship between the priorities and expectations.
—Do not terminate employment without having carried out the above steps and making very sure they have understood exactly what the situation is.

☐ Remember that discipline is defined as "training that builds and strengthens." When the leader applies this approach with diligence, integrity, and warmth, the number of unsatisfactory team members decreases significantly.

☐ It is rare to find a case of absenteeism if team members are well coached, are in the right job, know what is expected, and are empowered and truly led.

☐ The first hour of the first day on a new job exerts a profound influence on the team member. Make sure the team member:
—Feels expected and wanted.
—Is encouraged to ask questions and is given thoughtful and thorough answers.
—Feels part of a careful, thought-out orientation procedure.
—Is helped to thoroughly understand the new job.
—Ideally, learns of the uniqueness of the company and is helped to feel truly a part of it.

☐ Make sure the team is enlightened, empowered, energized, and enthusiastic.

THE TEAM CONCEPT

The excellent team has *tempo*, which I defined earlier as "the speed with which an organization identifies problems and opportunities and makes and implements decisions." But a real team has much, much more:

☐ A trust relationship among members of the team
☐ An attitude that is flexible, durable, open, growing, questing, vulnerable, and expective
☐ Clear, properly developed goals, objectives, and expectations
☐ A focus on strengths, the only tools an organization or an individual has
☐ A readiness to take on new and different challenges, problems, and opportunities
☐ Caring: the capacity, the desire to relate to people
☐ Accountability: feeling truly answerable for one's actions as a leader and team member
☐ Significance: uniqueness; realness
☐ Symbiosis: positive interaction conducive to synergy
☐ Synergy: the capacity to compound resources for positive results
☐ Candor, applied integrity
☐ Communication: shared meaning, shared understanding

Figure 12.1. The GROWTH path.

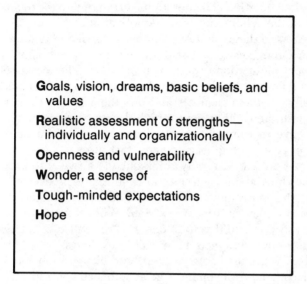

Goals, vision, dreams, basic beliefs, and
  values

Realistic assessment of strengths—
  individually and organizationally

Openness and vulnerability

Wonder, a sense of

Tough-minded expectations

Hope

THE TRUTH ABOUT MOTIVATION

We must get rid of the old idea that a leader can *give* motivation. All motivation is *self*-motivation. We simply cannot, and should not want to, install motivation externally. The excellent leader goes all out to provide the climate, the stimuli, and the example, but all *real* motivation is self-generated.

Only growing, actualized individuals can reach out beyond themselves in ways essential to true synergistic teams. No aggregate productivity can ever be more than mediocre unless the individuals in the group are experiencing purpose, direction, and fulfilled expectations.

An essential truth for leaders and team builders to grasp is this: *We can know and lead others only when we are progressively learning how to know and lead ourselves.* Self-discovery is a frequently neglected but crucial step. Remember, all growth is self-growth. *Grow* the example you want your team members to follow. As you chart your way through the rest of this chapter, on your personal quest, you may find it useful to study Figure 12.1, the growth path.

A JOURNEY OF SELF-DISCOVERY

To help you learn more about yourself and your motivation, I have prepared a set of ten questions, each broken down into a number of subquestions. The answers to each of the subquestions will enable you to answer the prime question. The questions correspond to the sequence shown in Figure 12.2, the cybernetic circle of motivation.

Your answers to these questions will be personal and unique. There can be no right or wrong answers. The purpose is to help you apply some practical ideas about motivation to your own situation. There is no set sequence or pattern to follow to become motivated. But certain elements are necessary. You can take these elements and mix them in any proportion or sequence you wish, and still achieve a high degree of motivation. Therefore, you do not have to complete the exercises in any particular order. If a certain section especially appeals to you, start there.

Take your time and carefully think out the answers to each question. The more you think about each question and really discover your thoughts and feelings, the more motivated you are likely to become. Do not feel compelled to complete this in one session. Work a section or two a day. There are ten sections, so if you do one a day it will take ten days. At the rate of two sections a day, you will finish in five days.

Remember, you must know yourself, and like yourself, before you can know and like others. And you must be able to lead yourself before you can lead others. I urge you to actually complete every question. The rewards can be enormous. Only through self-discovery can we progress on to self-fulfillment, self-actualization, and co-actualization. The person who follows such a growth path tremendously increases in ability to lead and to evoke the best from others. To do less is to fail to confront your possibilities.

We'll start with a list of some strengths to help start you thinking about your own. Of course, this is not an all-inclusive list. You will undoubtedly be able to think of other strengths unique to you once you start completing the sections.

Visionary	Emotional stamina
Affectionate	Humble
Hard-working	Thoughtful
Happy	Compassionate
Forgiving	Attractive
Disciplined	Diligent
Energetic	Tenacious
Fit	Sense of humor
Committed	Helpful
Tolerant	Outgoing
Cheerful	Resilient
Serene	Intelligent
Sincere	Emotionally stable
Focused	Self-starting

Figure 12.2. The cybernetic circle of motivation.

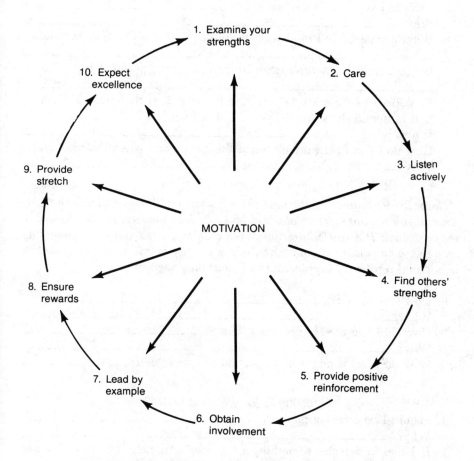

A Personal Pledge for the Tough-Minded Leader

1. I must learn more of my own strengths and learn to like, yes, and to love myself.
2. I must care enough about myself and others.
3. I must listen actively. Discover wants, needs, and problems.
4. I must care enough about others to look for and find their strengths.
5. I will provide positive reinforcement and build on strengths.
6. I will obtain involvement and input. Jointly agree on commitments.
7. I will lead with an example that I will be proud to have others follow.
8. I will ensure that rewards are provided in direct proportion to performance and that appropriate disciplinary steps are taken if commitments are not (under logical circumstances) met.
9. I will continue to stretch and discover who and what I really can be.
10. I will expect the best. Don't expect perfection. Do expect excellence!

Question 1. Who am I?

1. Five of my inner strengths are: _____
2. I can improve these strengths by: _____
3. I would like to add these strengths: _____
   Why? _____
4. What five needs do I most want to fulfill? [*List in order of importance.*]
   _____
5. Write a short paragraph describing: This is the person I think I am.
   _____
6. Look back to the answers you gave to items 1–4; then item 5. Do you
   find in item 5 the strengths you listed in items 1–4? _____
   If not, why? _____
7. How do I feel about myself when I'm happy *and* when I'm sad? _____
   Why? _____

[*Note: Before answering the next three questions, please be aware that the
term* love *does not refer to physical love. To love yourself is not egotistical
or conceited. It essentially means being able to accept and like yourself as
you are, being aware of your potential, as well as your limitations. It means
emotional resilience, suppleness, and constancy of purpose.*]

8. Do I love myself? _____
   Why? _____
9. How do I feel about answering item 8? _____
   Why? _____
10. Why do I feel it might be important to love myself? _____

Question 2. Why should I care?

1. Should I be a *caring* person? _____
   Why? _____
2. If I had to sacrifice something I felt was extremely important for the
   happiness of one of the following, would I?
   ☐ Parents   ☐ Friends
   ☐ Children   ☐ Business associates
   ☐ Spouse   ☐ Acquaintances
   ☐ Other relatives   ☐ Strangers
3. Why would I be willing to sacrifice or open myself to some of them and
   not others? _____
4. What would I be willing to do for someone I really cared about? [*List
   several things.*] _____
5. What would I not be willing to do? _____

6. Below is a list of traits. Which ones are found in a *caring* person?

Love	Openness and expectations
Sharing	Sincerity
Vulnerability	Helpfulness
Self-sacrificing	Humility

7. How many traits did I check?_____
   Which ones didn't I check?_____
   Why not?_____
8. [*Take another look at the traits in item 6. All these traits are needed if a person is to really care. Perhaps you're not able to feel all these traits operating with everyone.*] I have looked back at the list in item 2, and I can see all these traits in_____
9. How can I show my team members that I am a *caring* person? [*List five ways.*]_____
10. I have chosen one team member and one of the items I listed in item 9 just above. The person is_____and the method is_____. For one week I tried to show this person I care by using that method. These were the results:_____

Question 3. I listen, but . . .

1. Why do I feel it is important to really listen and hear what people say?

2. Here are five things that make it difficult for me to listen._____

3. Really *hearing* and *understanding* what a person says involves more than *listening*. I think these other things are also involved._____

4. Are there some people I don't listen to? [*Name two and tell why.*]

5. When I listen to someone, what should I be looking for?_____

6. What can I do to help myself become a better listener? [*List three things.*]_____

7. Feedback is one tool I can use to help me become a better listener. It involves the listener repeating back to the speaker the essence of what was said. Here is a recent incident or conversation when I used feedback, or could have:_____

8. Do I settle for "dialogue" (two or more people engaged in monologues) or go for communication (shared meaning, shared understanding)?

Question 4. How can finding and reinforcing other people's strengths help me?

1. Do I find it easy to see strengths in other people?_____
   Why?_____
2. I have chosen a team member (a co-worker or someone I lead). Here are five of that person's strengths [use skills or personality traits]:
   _____
3. Here are five of that person's unique talents or abilities (things he or she can do that I can't):_____
4. Did I have difficulty completing items 2 and 3?_____
   If so, I might consider getting to know that person better. How might I do this?_____
5. I will try following questions 2, 3, and 4 for other people at work and at home. Here's a list of the people and their strengths._____
   _____

   After a month, I will take another look at how I view them.

Question 5. Why do I need to reinforce those strengths?

1. How do I feel about giving people earned praise?_____
2. How do people react to my praise and compliments?_____
3. I tried complimenting the person I initially picked in question 4 above. This is the response I received:_____
4. I then tried complimenting the second group of people I listed in question 4 above, the others at work and at home. Which of their strengths did I compliment?_____
   How did they respond?_____
   After a month, how do I feel about these same people?_____
   (You may note some changes in their attitudes, and yours, that will surprise you.)_____
5. [Take another look at your list of people you selected for compliments and positive reinforcements. Consider the following and find examples of each]:
   a. How does caring about others help me?_____
   b. How does listening help me?_____
   c. How do finding and reinforcing others' strengths help me?_____

Question 6. Why get involved?

[Note: Involved means sharing, caring, relating, being vulnerable, asking, listening, hearing, suggesting.]

1. [Think about the last cause or project you were associated with and answer the following question]: Why did I get involved? [List the reasons.]_____

2. Could I be called an "involved" person?_____
   Why or why not?_____
3. This is how I would describe someone I know who is an "involved"
   person._____
4. Would I like to be more like the person I described?_____
   Why?_____
5. [*Imagine you are given responsibility for a major project at work. Consider this question*]: How would I go about getting my other project members involved? [*List the steps. Be sure to refer to your answers to item 1.*]
6. Could I use positive reinforcement to obtain someone's involvement?

   _____
   What kinds of reinforcement could I use?_____
7. Does my company give performance appraisals to let people know how they are doing?_____
   If so, how could these performance appraisals involve positive reinforcement? [*List three ways.*]_____
8. How could my team members as well as management personnel be involved in performance appraisals?_____
9. How could the following serve as an aid to positive reinforcement and involvement for my people?
   a. Compensation_____
   b. Incentives (a bonus plan, for instance)_____
   c. Company newsletter_____
   d. Promotion_____
   e. Other (something unique to your organization)_____

Question 7: Me? Lead by example?

1. Every day someone is influenced to follow my example, good or bad. Today, in this particular situation someone followed my lead. [*Describe the incident.*]_____
2. Do I *really* want to be a leader?_____
   Why?_____
3. What kind of example *do* I set for those around me? [*List some of your traits that other people have said they admired or disliked.*]_____

4. Am I happy with the way people see me?_____
5. If I could add or delete only one thing from the traits listed in item 3, what would it be?_____
6. Why did I choose this one particular trait?_____
7. I am imagining that I have only one week to live. I'm thinking of one person who looks to me for leadership, and these are the things I would like this person to remember about me:_____

8. I think I would like to make some changes in my leadership image, and I'll start with the person I picked in the preceding question. For one week, I'll make a conscious effort to *be* the person described. [*At the end of the week, refer to your list again; for each point, note whether you feel you succeeded and why.*]_____

Question 8. Are rewards necessary?

1. Are rewards and positive reinforcement the same?_____
2. I think a valid reward for the following might be:
   a. Meeting a stretching expectation_____
   b. Earning a promotion_____
   c. Excessive absence from work_____
   d. Stealing_____
3. What happens when a person is *not* rewarded promptly for either good or poor performance?_____
4. These five rewards are most meaningful to me:_____

5. What do I feel a team member's compensation should be based upon?

6. Do people in my organization know why they do or don't receive a raise?_____
   Why should they know?_____
7. How can I help ensure that my team members receive valid rewards for their work?_____

Question 9. Why do I need stretch?

1. Would I be satisfied to remain *exactly* as I am today for the rest of my life?_____
2. What does the word *growth* mean to me?_____
3. Is continuous personal growth necessary?_____
   Why?_____
4. Here are five ways in which I feel I have grown or stretched in the past year._____
5. How can personal goals or future plans help me grow?_____
6. Here are some of the adjectives I would use to describe what a goal should be:_____
7. There are two types of goals: short-term and long-range. Here is an example of each._____
8. I would like to achieve these three goals in the next year:_____

9. I would like to have achieved these three goals in the next five years:

10. I choose to concentrate on this one short-term goal._____
    These are the things I must do to accomplish it, and the time limit I
    set for each step:_____
11. At the end of a year, I accomplished these short-term goals:_____
    [*If you didn't reach any of those listed, list the reasons.*]_____
12. Now I will set these new goals:_____
13. Have I helped my people set goals for their work?_____
    Why might doing so help me?_____
14. Do I feel my organization should help its employees with career plan-
    ning?_____
    Why?_____
15. How would I go about helping one of my team members who has come
    to me for help and advice on career planning and personal growth?

Question 10. The best I can be . . .

1. What does excellence mean to me?_____
2. How do I know I am doing my *best?*_____
3. Why is it important to do my best?_____
4. What happens when someone expects me to do my best?_____
5. What happens when I expect others to do their best?_____
6. What happens when someone expects my worst or second best?_____
7. What positive G forces stimulate me the most?_____

The key to greater personal motivation lies *within you.* It cannot be
handed to you by any other person. There are some steps you can learn
that will give you the rewards you desire, and the preceding questions have
been designed to help you master them. All ten steps are important.

Continue to provide room for stretch in your life and in the lives of
those around you. You will be surprised to discover new and exciting things
about who you are and can be. This will make it possible for you to reach
out and help others discover possibilities that will enable them to grow also.
This is one of the finest tributes you can give another person: the ability to
see who the person *is* and who he or she *can be.*

LEADERSHIP IN THE TWENTY-FIRST CENTURY

How can we preserve our aspirations and at the same time develop the toughness of mind and spirit to face the fact that there are no easy victories? One is a tough-minded recognition that the fight for a better world is a long one.

JOHN GARDNER
NO EASY VICTORIES

From right and left we hear cries of gloom and doom about the future of American corporations. Quick-fix artists and one-minute solutions abound. Attempts to understand and emulate the "productive genius" of

*The above excerpt from *No Easy Victories* is copyright © 1969 by John W. Gardner. Reprinted by permission of Harper & Row, Publishers, Inc.

the Japanese proliferate like rabbits. Theories X, Y, and Z ebb and flow. Often the picture seems to show many famous corporations as stumbling giants. At a premium are leaders with vision, courage, integrity, tenacity, energy, and insight into the exciting and revolutionary possibilities of the future. One of the greatest needs for today's leaders is the need to anticipate change and prepare for the future rather than fight it.

Management leaders in generations to come will not be people who have merely mastered a discipline or achieved a graduate degree or two. They will not be financiers, supersalespersons, or experts at analysis. They will be people who are able to inspire others, who can weld together many individuals of wide and diverse experiences and abilities into cohesive groups with singleness of purpose.

INTEGRITY THAT PERVADES AND SUFFUSES

The quality of our minds will only be as good as the quality or integrity of our beliefs and values. Indeed, the total value of all we accomplish is the sum of the values between our ears.

Are we laying our ethics and dignity aside too often, in the seemingly never-ending rush for greater pleasure, more spare time, and more money? Are businesspeople helping the country's integrity slip backward into lethargy? Without the positive guidelines and governors that are imposed by personal integrity, could we find ourselves in an atmosphere of self-centered greed? Have we been knocked off base by the greed inherent in large-scale scandals (for example, the Wall Street insider trading crimes of 1987)?

Is there, in fact, any real integrity in any business transaction that is not accompanied or followed up by excellent service? Greed and excellence of service simply do not mesh. The tough-minded leader takes steps to ensure that the organization is guided by *crystal-clear ethics criteria in all areas and at all levels.* These are my suggestions:

1. I will live by the premise that to perpetuate my business and to be a good executive, I must make the best-quality product possible at minimum cost, market it competitively, and achieve the optimum legitimate profit in return.
2. I will recognize that my greatest resources in business are my team members and my friends.
3. I will refuse to take advantage of a situation that will reflect adversely on the reputation of my company.
4. I will refuse to take any advantage of a business opportunity if it may entail a violation of the morals, ethics, and laws of justice that I personally believe to be the foundation of our society.

5. I will endeavor always to look for the positive, constructive, and developmental answers to problems concerning my team members. I will demonstrate confidence in times of crisis.
6. I will refuse to stretch honesty to the last letter of the law; my intention is more important than the act.
7. I will practice—within the limits of wisdom—constructive candor, warm understanding, and helpful assistance to all who ask it.
8. I will confront my problems honestly and squarely, talking them out and solving them to the best of my knowledge and ability. I will ask, listen, and *hear*.
9. I will recognize that both competition and cooperation built our country and that I must help to perpetuate these desirable attributes of our society for the future.
10. I will believe that the Ten Commandments are the supreme laws that should guide and inspire me.

Tough-minded leaders view all this in perspective. They know that the ultimate price must somehow be paid. They know that phonies finish last! Unless a person builds a life on a value system rooted in daring, caring, and sharing, he or she will early drift away into a phony, meaningless existence.

Real men and women who want to lead real and renewing lives will be guided by these principles:

Serve much.
Care much.
Dare much.
Share much.
Stretch much.
Expect much.
Give much.
Live much.
Love much.
Grow much.
Empower and renew much.
Experiment much.
Seek challenges and obstacles.
Have a sense of wonder.
Have a specific program of physical, mental, and spiritual fitness.
Make the quantum leap from judging others on the basis of their weaknesses
    to evaluating them according to their current and potential strengths.

Truth and ethics can be enormously powerful when they are effectively focused and practiced. Some helpful thoughts for the positive G force leader include:

- [ ] Dwell on what a person can do, and should do, rather than on how badly they have done or may do.
- [ ] Sporadic or unplanned abrasiveness can be cruel.
- [ ] Scrupulously avoid the temptation to develop whipping boys or scapegoats. Make sure candor and openness are rewarded.
- [ ] Recognize that you gain confidence and courage every time you meet head on a situation that you were previously afraid of.
- [ ] Be sincere. Remember that real warmth and graciousness can't be cultivated as long as you are concerned primarily with yourself.
- [ ] Give earned compliments freely. Learn to relish this privilege.
- [ ] Don't blame anyone else for what you are not, but be grateful to those who have helped you become what you are.
- [ ] Try to prove yourself only through positive action. If you have been trying to impress people by downsizing others, quit it!
- [ ] Have the courage to change what can be changed, the serenity to accept that which can't, and the wisdom to know the difference.
- [ ] Be compassionate.

How can the leader achieve *personal* tooling for integrity? Find the effective, self-disciplined practitioner and you will likely find a person who:

Meets commitments and *gives* loyalty
Follows a realistic schedule
Is physically, mentally, and spiritually fit
Understands and feels good about self
Is a strong individual (*integrity* and *strength* mean the same)
Operates by results, not activity
Scrupulously insists on the truth
Conducts a periodic self-inventory and maximizes own strengths
Knows true creativity is impossible without hard work and followthrough
Develops pace, tempo, and stamina
Can identify and eliminate trivia
Has happy domestic relations
Usually achieves empathy
Shuns political infighting
Fosters, exemplifies, and builds communicative networking
Does not tolerate continued flabby methods in others
Confronts difficulties squarely

Gets to the heart of the problems and talks them out
Is totally intolerant of lack of integrity

Integrity is not just a nice word. It is the essence, the sum and substance of all that is worthwhile.

BECOME A BIG PERSON

The leaders of today and tomorrow must be big people. By this I am not referring to physical height. Rather, I mean leaders whose goals, vision, dreams, commitment, and dedication loom large. In *"What Works for Me"*: *Sixteen CEOs Talk About Their Careers and Commitments*, Thomas R. Horton quotes Richard A. Zimmerman, chairman and CEO of Hershey Foods:

> *Among the CEOs I know, the most successful ones have a very positive outlook.* Every CEO has to be a cheerleader. *At times you may feel that you can list a series of disaster scenarios for your company, and certainly you are in the best position to do that; still, you have to be a cheerleader at least part of the time. . . . OK, we know it is going to be tough, but let's get at it! You need always to be encouraging and perhaps that is one of the most admired attributes that I see in most CEOs.*[1]

And elsewhere,

> *It is important to always have that vision of where you want to go. And most good CEOs always have that vision.*[2]

Marisa Bellisario, CEO of Italtel Societá Italiana Telecommunicazioni, believes:

> *Always in some way I tend to take on more. . . . Whenever I have taken a job, I never thought I couldn't make it.*[3]

Tough-minded leaders feel, demonstrate, and express supreme self-confidence! They are comfortable with the sharing of power, authority, and beliefs.

Portia Isaacson, CEO of Intellisys, says:

1. (New York: Random House, 1986).
2. Ibid.
3. Ibid.

I am sure that to many people the act of my starting up Intellisys is equally bizarre. . . . I could fail really visibly, but I guess I don't care. I don't think about that at all. *It simply does not occur to me that we could fail.*[4]

Tough-minded executives should be hungry for a deep understanding of "positive thinking." It is much more than a catch-phrase. Leaders must consider the specific implications it has for the leader of the future. Robert H. Waterman, Jr. says:

An attitude some call FUD—fear, uncertainty, and doubt—is the nemesis of the tough-minded optimism that sustains renewal.[5]

Waterman also says:

IBM's no-layoff, full-employment policy, like the company itself, is tough-minded optimism in action. *It is based on respect for the individual, a tenet deeply imbedded in the company's culture and central to all management decision making.*[6]

As the massive, pivotal shift from the G forces of the past to the G forces of the future unfolds, the greatest premium will always be *you* the *leaders*. All growth is self-growth. All positive G teams are led to self-management. What you *are* can thunder so loud, they'll *want* to hear what you say!

Warren Bennis believes that:

First, true leaders lead fully integrated lives, *in which their careers and their personal lives fit seamlessly and harmoniously together.*[7]

LEAD AND MANAGE CHANGE

Tough-minded leaders know that changes in business and the world in general are inevitable, and they relish them! They anticipate the unfolding of the future, plan for it, and set trends. They require and encourage a climate conducive to innovation in all facets of the business. Above all, they are *change agents*. They recognize that a positive G-force culture depends on certain pivotal changes:

4. Ibid.
5. Robert H. Waterman, Jr., *The Renewal Factor: How the Best Get and Keep the Competitive Edge* (New York: Bantam, 1987).
6. Ibid.
7. Bennis and Burt Nanus, *Leaders* (New York: Harper & Row, Publishers, Inc., 1985).

1. *Relate compensation to performance.* Tough-minded leaders believe that providing rewards for seniority, long hours, racial or ethnic background, formal education, and old-school ties denies the dignity and worth of the individual. They care too much for people not to expect their best and pay them for results.

2. *Generate enthusiasm.* These leaders retain and expand their sense of wonder. They let their love of life, their acquired exuberance *show.* They believe it is crucial to "get things done and have a lot of fun" and know the two things are indivisible. They share life, love, and laughter with their team.

3. *Be not deterred by small people.* Leaders are not deterred by small and petty thinkers. They know what they want and what the organization needs. They secure maximum involvement and participation from their team, and move ahead resolutely toward the actual practice of management by integrity and empowerment.

4. *Build on strengths.* While tough-minded leaders recognize that they, like all people, have weaknesses, their primary concern is *strengths.* They know it is strengths, not weaknesses, that will make their organizations thrive.

5. *Remember that expectations are everything.* Leaders *stretch* their people, but never expect more from any person than that person is capable of performing. They often expect more than the people themselves believe they can accomplish. This is their key for developing confidence in individuals and helping them obtain a maximum feeling of accomplishment and empowerment. They know that expectations are the key to all happenings.

6. *Remain goal oriented.* Since a straight line is the shortest distance between two points, leaders know they must have some future point clearly in mind or they will dissipate their efforts.

7. *Practice leadership.* Real leaders lead as they would like to be led. Their style is passionate rather than passive. They walk in front of the flock. Like a compass, they provide direction, guidance, and magnetic pull.

8. *Foster significance.* Leaders know people can truly live and grow only if they feel *real*, if they can experience faith, hope, love, and gratitude. The two greatest contributions to feelings of significance are clear, stretching expectations, and growing awareness of strengths.

9. *Believe in intuition.* Tough-minded leaders relish the freedom to be subjective while they seek out all the objective information that can help them make correct and profitable decisions. They know that courage and logic are key components of intuition, and that intuition is really the ability to make spontaneous decisions, to take risks, to gamble on calculated vulnerability.

> *Every man knows that in his work he does his best*
> *and accomplishes most when he has attained a*
> *proficiency that enables him to work intuitively.*
> *That is, there are things which we come to know so*
> *well (the product of study and discipline, ergo,*
> *logic) that we do not know how we know them.*
> *Perhaps we live best and do things best when we are*
> *not too conscious of how and why we do them.*
> ALBERT EINSTEIN

VALUES MANIFESTO FOR TOUGH-MINDED LEADERS

These are some things that real leaders believe in and practice every day of their lives.

1. *Openness and emotional vulnerability.* Leaders let other people *in* and let themselves out. They believe that the absence of defensiveness is an indication of strength and management maturity. An undue concern for safety and comfort reverses growth and creates apathy.

2. *Warmth.* Leaders reach out to people; they do not simply sit back and wait. They demonstrate caring and concern. Their voices and manners project relaxation and positive concern.

3. *Consistency.* Leaders meet commitments, keep their word, and can be relied upon. They expect the same from others.

4. *Unity.* Leaders have a fused and focused oneness of purpose, effort, and direction.

5. *Caring.* Leaders want others to grow and benefit. They believe *love* is the toughest-minded emotion in the world.

6. *Positive listening.* Leaders are *positive* listeners. They keep an open and flexible mind. Since they encourage creativity within their organization, they listen positively to ideas that are presented, trying to discover ways that will work. Above all, they *hear.*

7. *Unsatisfaction.* Leaders are hungry for improvement, growth, and a better way. They have a fanatical commitment to constantly stretching and reaching for the best.

8. *Flexibility.* Leaders abhor rigidity in all forms. They know hardness and weakness are usually synonymous. Their minds are resilient and supple.

9. *Giving.* Leaders believe that the more people put into—or give—to life and their work, the more they receive. Also, giving yields more real pleasure. They relish giving earned praise! They know that go-getters ultimately get *got.*

10. *Involvement.* Leaders seek the involvement of their people in developing their goals and plans, not only because they want to use all the talents within their organization, but also because they know that people will be more committed to meeting these objectives if they have a part in determining them.

11. *Tolerance of mistakes.* Leaders have the courage to let people make mistakes. They even encourage it! They recognize that people learn by doing and so if they do anything they are going to make mistakes. By recognizing this, they also delegate better.

12. *Values.* Leaders realize values should be precision instruments that inspire, unify, and stretch. They believe that leaders who are value *driven* are not leaders at all; they are pushers. True leaders are value *led*.

13. *Psychological wages.* Leaders provide for a psychic as well as a real wage for their people because they recognize psychological as well as physical needs. Their focus is always on the whole person.

14. *Simplicity.* Leaders constantly strive to make the complex simple. They know settling for a complex solution is settling for second best. They have the ability to deal with complexity, ambiguity, and uncertainty. They prefer the simple and tough to the complex and easy.

15. *Time.* Leaders guard their time preciously and allot it to key areas where it will produce the greatest impact. Since there are so many stretching goals to achieve, they concentrate their time and energy on doing one thing at a time and doing first things first. They set priorities and stick to them even if it means secondary things do not get done at all.

16. *The winning formula.* Integrity plus quality plus service says it all. Leaders create customer satisfaction through quality, productivity, people, and ideas.

17. *An open mind.* An open mind can grow. A closed mind dies. Where there is an open mind, there will always be a frontier.

18. *Development of people.* Leaders believe and live the concept that the development of people, as a whole and in depth, pays real dividends to both the business and the individual. They know this is the alpha and omega of the great organization of the future.

19. *Self-discipline.* Leaders practice self-discipline in every dimension of their lives.

20. *Physical fitness.* Leaders recognize that developing maximum physical fitness is an important requisite of mental health and acuity. Such fitness is not self-indulgence but part of an executive's obligation to business, team members, and family.

21. *Enjoyment of life.* Leaders enjoy life—and people know it! Dour, scowling, formidable executives only succeed in compressing, repressing, and depressing their team members.

22. *Broad perspective.* Leaders' interests and activities may range glob-

ally. Truly broad-gauge leaders read widely and have their own personal-development program. They believe that a broad and eclectic fund of knowledge makes for not only a better generalist, but also a better specialist. They see the broad picture, look beyond their own specialty or function to think in terms of the customer—the ultimate reason for their jobs.

23. *Faith in self and others.* Leaders believe we are the sum of our strengths and that the only *real* things to search for and believe in are the strengths of ourselves and others. They *assume* there is positive evidence of strengths that are still unseen.

24. *Vision.* Vision provides the basic energy, lift, and stretch for pulling the organization toward the future. Positive people will intuitively respond to a leader's positive dreams.

25. *Positive thinking.* Leaders believe negativism is never justified. They know that there are plus and minus elements in many situations but that the minus areas can be made into pluses.

26. *Desire to learn.* Leaders cultivate a curiosity for new dimensions of knowledge and resist efforts to predicate plans on past and present knowledge only. They do not confuse wit or intelligence with wisdom, and they strive steadily for greater wisdom. They are life-long learners. They cultivate a perpetual sense of wonder.

27. *Enjoyment of work.* Leaders know that life without work is a short-cut to deterioration, that hard positive work is one of life's great renewing agents. They relish feelings of accomplishment. They are literally hungry for new obstacles, difficulties, and strength-building confrontations.

28. *Enrichment of others.* Leaders are proud of the free enterprise way of life and seek to enrich the lives of others by the richness of their own.

29. *Integrity.* Leaders *live* integrity, instead of relying on preachments and pointing fingers. They know that leadership by integrity is realistic and workable; that in reality, there is no fit substitute for it.

30. *Results, not activity.* Excellent leaders concentrate on results rather than activity. They measure the performance of their team members in terms of results and their contribution to company objectives. They believe that people are on the payroll for only one reason—to make a significant contribution to company objectives and to *grow*. They believe one must do the job or get out of it.

31. *Candor.* Leaders practice truth rigorously and reflect a true warmth of feeling toward their associates. They have the guts to say what ought to be said. They practice positive warmth in the process.

32. *Management by example.* Leaders know that the actions of a responsible leader are contagious, and that there is virtually no limit to potential accomplishment if leaders set the example of looking for strengths and expecting the best.

33. *A clear philosophy.* Leaders make sure that their organization's phi-

losophy and objectives are researched, developed, and clearly communicated. They believe the philosophy must pervade and saturate everything in the organization and form the foundation of its culture.

34. *Accountability*. Leaders believe people are more efficient and happier when they understand clearly what results are expected of them and when they are involved in determining these results.

35. *Purpose and direction*. Leaders are visionaries. They know that all team members will contribute and receive more if they are helped to develop clear feelings of purpose, direction, dignity, and expectations. They provide direction, not directions. They explain very thoroughly what they want, but leave the how up to their team members.

36. *Expectations of excellence*. Leaders know that perhaps the finest gift you can give another person is the gift of a stretching expectation based on a never-ending search for that person's strengths.

37. *Laserlike focus*. Leaders compare the average group of people on one hand and their untapped possibilities on the other to the difference between an ordinary room full of diffused particles of light and the laser beam with its mind-boggling propensities and possibilities. They know the answer is:

Vision + Focus + Action = The G Forces of the Future

CHAPTER **14**

LEADERSHIP BY RENEWAL

The central purpose of managing by renewal is to make effective use of the strengths of the organization to fulfill organizational dreams. Computerized strengths banks can facilitate mind-boggling innovations during the turbulent decade ahead.

Humans are delightful skinfuls of variables. They are unpredictable, unique, and important. How can we get to know people quickly and well? One important way is to seek diligently to discover their strengths, because each person is the *sum of these strengths.* Weaknesses are only missing strengths; they only confuse us and indicate what the other person is *not.* How can we help people to feel significant and worthwhile? One of the best ways is to constantly *look* for and *expect* their best. In this way we begin to employ the principle of high expectations. Second-rate expectations

133

suggest second-rate regard for others. First-rate expectations say clearly and distinctly, "I think you are first-rate. I value you."

The central premise here is that we can best help people discover themselves, etch out their uniqueness and individuality, and grow in confidence and significance when we care enough—in the real tough-minded and tenderhearted sense—to help them become all they can be. When we care enough to:

Constantly look for their best
Consistently expect their best
Compensate them in relation to their performance
Provide a vision and expective focus

THE NEED FOR SIGNIFICANCE
In the on-the-job sense, the usual undesirable indices—such as turnover, absenteeism, and low morale—would be vastly reduced if all team members felt more significant and useful.

It is important to understand the difference between self-esteem and significance. You might have a reasonable measure of self-esteem, but still feel underchallenged, underused, and underactualized, and therefore less than fully significant.

Paul "Bear" Bryant, the legendary football coach at the University of Alabama, said there are five things that winning team members need to know:

1. Tell me what you expect from me.
2. Give me an opportunity to perform.
3. Let me know how I'm getting along.
4. Give me guidance where I need it.
5. Reward me according to my contribution.

Of course, we need love and respect from others, but we won't feel fully *significant* unless our conscience tells us we are using and constructively realizing our possibilities.

THE SEVEN PHASES OF THE SYSTEM
Now let's examine the seven phases that constitute the mechanisms of the system of leadership by renewal. Look back at Figure 6.1, which illustrates these seven phases. Here I will touch on just a few of the key elements that are required for active operation. The discussion can serve as a basis for beginning a strengths-management system in your organization.

Phase 1. Strengths Identification

Here the goal is to determine the reality of the individuals, their strengths, and thus determine the real capacity and potential of the organization. To accomplish this, implement these three steps:

1. Complete individual inventories of *all* members of the team. Search for real and demonstrated strengths as well as those hoped for.
2. List "victories"—past experiences where people achieved a measure of what they hoped for.
3. List individual objectives and relate them to job objectives. These should indicate strengths that can contribute directly to job results.

I firmly believe that the bottom line—which is the most unerring indication of strengths deployment—will be greatly improved when leaders make an organizational investment in helping all team members really think through and work out personal objectives for themselves.

When you conduct interviews, listen for strengths. Don't get bogged down and preoccupied with weaknesses.

Phase 2. Strengths Classification

Here you are working to determine precisely what the relative kinds and types of strengths are. This is where a computerized strengths bank really pays for itself.

☐ Prepare anecdotal records listing key strengths of your team members. A primary step here is to ask the group to provide you with a list of their strengths classified according to their own priorities.
☐ Categorize and computerize the inventories for practical and applied use. Look for:
Decision-making strengths: evaluation skills
Problem-solving strengths: analytical skills
Face-to-face strengths: communication skills
☐ List degrees of strengths, from major to minor. It is important to know weaknesses so that you can determine what additional strengths are needed or what is needed to develop existing strengths further.
☐ Develop strengths software.

Phase 3. Strengths Development

Policies, procedures, and practices are designed to increase the strengths and the effectiveness of all personnel, in terms of performance. To develop team members' strengths to the maximum, take these steps:

☐ Prepare and disseminate a companywide philosophy stressing strengths development.
☐ Conduct research to determine training and development needs and specific requirements.
☐ Prepare a thoughtful strengths-development plan.
☐ Implement the plan. For example, you might set up:
  Computerized strength banks and strengths-access software
  Specifically designed modules
  Assessment centers
  Career path planning
  Carefully designed assignment of position and job content
  Provision of specific strengths-actualization information
  Personnel planning

You cannot develop mechanistic elements such as equipment, paper, floorspace, and written processes. You can develop only living human strengths.

Phase 4. Assignment of Strengths

The implications here for high individual and organizational morale are enormous. Essentially, the proper and full use of their strengths is the greatest single need of people. Making the right hiring decisions can mean the difference between success and failure of the company. The challenge is to find people whose strengths you need and put them in positions where they can use them. You're looking for three different kinds of strengths:

1. *Demonstrated and tested strengths.* In actuality, this is what people are paid for. This is *performance!* Use these strengths where they will be the most effective in helping both the individual and the company meet goals.
2. *Suspected strengths.* These can be verified and rewarded only by stretching assignments.
3. *Expected strengths.* These help employees discover who they are, what they can be, and what they can do; this is one practical way to describe and understand the process of leadership.

Be prepared to depart from basing assignments on mechanistic assumptions of the traditional roles of women, men, minorities, or other groups. Shift from role orientation to goal orientation, thus bringing strengths fully to bear. Develop imaginative computer software in your computerized strengths bank that can give you enormous help in applying these principles.

Phase 5. Synergy and Expectations

True synergy is invariably the product of a wise blend of strengths. The wisdom of this blend is usually in direct proportion to the clarity, logic, and relevance of the expectations developed. Here are three suggestions for developing your expectation instruments, thus bringing your team members together:

1. *Positive accountability provisions.* The proper use of accountability is always to focus on and maximize the use of strengths, never to become preoccupied with weaknesses.
2. *Results expected.* In other words, statements of what you want done. Such commitments should be products of sound discussion and involvement sessions.
3. *Performance standards.* These will help determine how well the job should be done.

Here you will be involved in training and counseling your human resources. Some key requirements of effective coaching are:

☐ *Positive listening.* Make sure you really *hear* their wants, needs, and problems.
☐ *Vulnerability and openness.* We grow and discover new capacities and abilities only when we are vulnerable and open.
☐ *Flexibility and versatility.* Rigidity is like rigor mortis. Life and growth are synonymous with supple attitudes and practices.

In this phase, the principle of high expectations comes alive. In all your interactions with your team members, remember these guidelines:

☐ *Express caring.* Keep trying to evoke the best in others. To do less is to indicate lack of caring.
☐ *Motivate.* Help clarify the individual's motives (objectives) and relate them to the motives (objectives) of the organization.
☐ *Clarify.* Emphasize each individual's strengths. Discover the renewing pleasure of giving earned praise consistently and zestfully.
☐ *Stretch.* Require the individual to reach deeply within to find the strengths to increase quality or quantity of performance.
☐ *Build teamwork and real self-esteem.* We can truly respect ourselves and reach out cooperatively to others only when we feel we are doing reasonably tough or difficult things.

Although the end results of such synergy are objective measurements (for example, money), the capacity to generate the optimum measure of these results stems directly from, and in proportion to, the use of subjective strengths like thought, emotions, and attitude.

Phase 6. Strengths Measurement

Measure the strengths of people, money, materials, time, and space by overhauling all policies, procedures, processes, practices, and programs to reflect strengths emphasis. This emphasis should be incorporated into the following:

☐ *Annual reports.* Describe new possibilities inherent in the resources (people, money, materials, time, and space) of the organization.

☐ *Budgets and forecasts.* Include possibility thinking, which moves beyond the typical comparisons with past achievements.

☐ *Profit plans.* Organization manuals.

☐ *Policy manuals.* Make sure that all standard operating policies and procedures are redesigned and rewritten to reflect strengths emphasis.

☐ *Progress reports.* Stress progress toward objectives rather than weaknesses or deviations.

☐ *Strength audits.* Systematically measure actual performance compared to estimated possibilities.

☐ *Manpower inventories.* Reflect current and projected estimates of strengths resources. (In reality, the only resources of an organization are its strengths.)

☐ *Visual inspection.*

☐ *Memoranda.*

☐ *Committees.* Be sure all discussions, plans, and actions make the shift from "trouble shooting" to "possibility shooting."

☐ *Individual service standards.* Build into every position a prioritized component that stresses service as basic to all else.

Phase 7. Control of Strengths

It is virtually redundant to say "control of strengths" because control by its very definition in the TML lexicon is the focused, expected, and monitored utilization of strengths to achieve targeted results. Control need not be even remotely coercive, repressive, or stultifying. Rather it must derive from focus, stretch, expectiveness, and other elements that follow:

☐ *Positive listening.* The terms *positive* and *strength* are synonymous, just as *negative* and *weakness* are. We can listen positively only if we feel secure in our awareness of our own strength.

☐ *Compensation.* This is related directly to demonstrated strengths—results.

☐   *Performance appraisal.* Managerial assessments, incident files, and face-to-face interaction that build on strengths rather than focus on weaknesses.

Many fine organizations are beginning to exemplify this strengths paradigm in a preliminary way. In his book, *People Power* (1988), John Noe describes the system he is employing in his company, Industrial Housekeeping Management Systems, Inc.:

> *The first step was to analyze every position in terms of the strengths needed and arrive at a profile of the person who would be successful in the position. Then, we began to systematically evaluate each applicant through the use of resume, employment application, personality assessment tools, interviews with questions targeted at the applicant's weaknesses, and references, and to determine how the individual would complement those who were already employees or who would be members of the newly formed team. We selected our management employees based on the known probability that they would succeed.*

BEYOND ORGANIZATIONAL DEVELOPMENT
TO ORGANIZATIONAL RENEWAL

If you still have any doubts about the power of expectation, you may be interested in this fascinating experiment, described by consultant Harold McAlindon, a long-time colleague:

> *Organization actualization [renewal] builds and extends the principles of organization development. A climate of high expectations, for example, is established in the actualizing organization.*
>
> *The importance of high expectations in achieving a person's potential was demonstrated at one school. There, teachers were advised that a unique test had been devised, one that could spot a youngster who was about to "bloom" intellectually. In reality no such test existed. The fake test was called the Harvard Test of Inflected Acquisition, but it was actually an unfamiliar and little-used standard test of intelligence.*
>
> *The teachers were asked to give this test and were advised that the top 20 percent would be the children about ready to surge ahead, regardless of their development to date. The teachers did not see the actual scores, which were irrelevant anyway. Instead, they were given the names of the top 20 percent group and told to expect rapid intellectual growth and development. In reality the names were chosen by random selection.*
>
> *A year later the same children were tested. The results were interesting. Dramatic increases on test scores were found in the 20 percent*

group. Simply because teachers were told to expect progress with certain children, progress took place. Gains in I.Q. scores were as great as 50 percent in a single year. No special techniques were given the teachers to influence this change. No special tools or materials were provided. The only difference was in the attitude of the teacher. The teacher expected growth and improvement and got it.[1]

A RENEWING PHILOSOPHY

The Employee Bill of Rights of Saga Administrative Corporation guarantees team members:

1. The right to give and receive feedback.
2. The right of fair treatment in every area of work experience.
3. The right to basic dignity, respect, and personal identity as a human being.
4. The right to a style of management that enhances self-esteem and dignity as a person.
5. The right to have the opportunity for a meaningful job for which they are qualified.
6. The right to be consulted and involved in those decisions that relate to the employee's job.
7. The right to be involved in social action programs.
8. The right to set their own work goals.
9. The right to set their own lifestyle.
10. The right to be creative in the performance of the task and in the fulfillment of the daily goals.
11. The right to fair compensation for their efforts.
12. The right to work hard to develop in a way that enables them to meet new challenges.
13. The right to be coached, assisted, and helped in the achievement of their goals.
14. The right to an optimistic, trusting, caring relationship in their work environment.

1. *Getting the Most Out of Your Job and Your Organization*—a collection of reprints from *Supervisory Management* (New York: AMACOM, 1980).

## CHAPTER 15

LEAD BY EXAMPLE

The leader is the evangelist for the dream.
DAVE PATTERSON, APPLE COMPUTER

The last thing organizations need is leaders who are diffident, tentative, hesitant, or submissive. They need leaders who will confront tough issues and tough challenges. When your team members look at you, what do they see? Are you enjoying life? Do you radiate vitality, well-being, and excitement? Are you a walking example of these leadership traits?

☐ Impatience for results.
☐ A sense of purpose. Leaders know what they are *for*, what they want to get done. Their priorities are vision, focus, action.
☐ A positive approach to problems.
☐ The feeling that a problem can be solved until proved otherwise.
☐ Practical judgment. They see the balance among people, money, materials, time, and space.

141

☐ Familiarity with the "six honest serving men": what, where, when, who, how, and why.
☐ Courage and candor.
☐ A knowledge that all people need recognition, belonging, security, opportunity, and significance.
☐ Acceptance of the fact that all projects of any significance involve planning, organization, coordination, direction, and control.
☐ A tough, durable mind that refuses to dissipate mental, physical, and emotional energy on negative thinking.
☐ A continuous search for strengths.
☐ A zest for life, love, and wholeness.
☐ A style that gives team members in the organization power to initiate and sustain efforts based on the integrity of an idea.
☐ Probability thinking at all levels.
☐ Belief in intuition—gut feelings—and followthrough.

THE POWER OF TRANSCENDENT GOALS

To fully plumb the possibilities of leading by example, I challenge you to find yourself by losing yourself in commitment to strong, stretching, powerful, tough ideas. No team ever finishes ahead of its leader. A true responsive leader must dare to stand out from the crowd.

Let's take an example from the world of sports. Tom Davis is the coach of the University of Iowa basketball team. Here Marc Hansen, sports columnist for the *Des Moines Register*, offers some observations on how Davis's firm, upbeat leadership style makes him stand out:

If Tom Davis isn't the most positive, controlled college basketball coach in the country, he's in the top five. His players, he says, face enough negative feedback daily—from the students, the media, and the fans— without his adding to the surplus. As Davis sees it, his job is to "deflect" the criticisms and the pressures. He also wants to eliminate the unrealistic expectations that accompany a successful program—that's why you'll rarely hear Davis go overboard in his praise of his best players and especially of incoming recruits. It seems to work. In all his years as a coach for a major college team, Davis has never lost a first-round NCAA tournament game. That isn't to say he never loses his temper or scolds his players. He does, but never in public and never for protracted periods. After the University of Iowa lost an emotion-charged overtime game to Iowa State in Ames last season, Davis locked the dressing room door and administered a severe verbal spanking. Even the players were taken aback. But after a tense few minutes, Davis paused and said, "Okay, this one's over, it's finished. Let's put it behind us." With

that, he opened the door, walked to his postgame news conference—
calm, composed and, as always, positive.

The single most important task of leadership is to inspire commitment
to a cause greater than self, commitment to a goal that transcends material
considerations. Style and substance are not mutually exclusive. Leadership
style in action *is* substance!

IDEALISM OR REALISM?

One day in Boston, where I was presenting a seminar
on tough-minded management, a professor from the
Harvard Business School joined me at the coffee break.
"Joe," he said, "I had expected you to be an intensely
practical guy, but I must say you sound to me more
like an idealist."

"Thanks."

"I didn't mean that as a compliment," he quickly
said; "I paid to learn some *practical* management
skills."

With a smile, I said, "Would you mind picking
up on this conversation with me when the day is over?
I'd really like to know what you think then."

When the seminar was completed at about 4:30,
we sat down together to talk some more. I will always
remember the excellence and clarity with which he
expressed his opinion.

"I think I've got it figured out. There's nothing
more impractical than an idealist with *impractical*
ideals, but there is nothing *more* practical than an
idealist with *practical ideals.*"

William Ouchi says:

That small spark of desire to change typically comes from a key person
who cares sufficiently about the organization to invest the time, energy
and risk in taking leadership. A manager who chooses to lead his de-
partment, division or company in a new direction can produce suffi-
cient trust and sufficient incentive for change to sustain the process for
some period, perhaps a year. If, during this period, some signs of prog-

Figure 15.1. Expective life planning instrument.

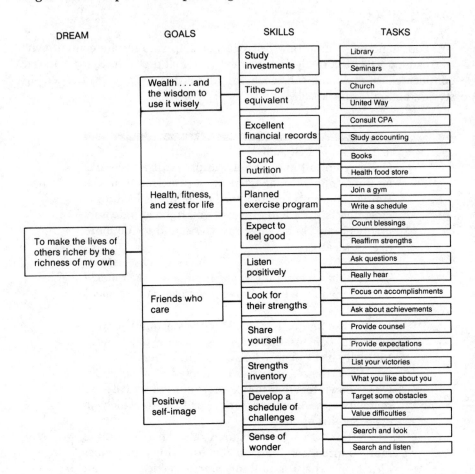

ress can be discerned by the followers, then the process of change will become nearly self-sustaining.[1]

To create that kind of climate, to inspire others with your vision, you must first take the time to clarify your own goals.

Figure 15.1 lays out a schematic PERT approach and presents a dream, some goals, some skills, and some tasks. The items shown in the figure are

1. *Theory Z* (Reading, Mass.: Addison-Wesley, © 1981). Excerpt is from page 99. Reprinted with permission of Addison-Wesley Publishing Co., Inc.

intended only as food for thought. This is simply a model, and I suggest that you set up your own version of this format, adding the components of your *own* dream, goals, skills, and tasks.

Once you have determined your dream and set out goals, skills, and tasks, you have only stated intentions. Now you need some specifics to enable you to follow through. Figure 15.2 illustrates an action plan; use it for each goal indicated in your dream. More about this figure in Chapter 18.

Next, it is important to monitor your progress to be sure that you are making steady and consistent gain. The planning control sheet in Figure 15.3 will help you stay on target.

A CORPORATE EXAMPLE

We Believe in the Dignity of the Individual

However large or complex a business may be, its work is still done by people. Each person involved is a unique human being, with pride, needs, values and innate personal worth. For us to succeed we must operate in a climate of openness and trust, in which each of us freely grants others the same respect, cooperation and decency we seek for ourselves.

BORG-WARNER CORPORATION

LOVE—IS IT TOO BIG FOR YOU?

Leadership *is* an example! Effective leaders deliberately set an example of what they expect and want from team members. If quality and service are truly important to you, exemplify quality and service in all you say, do, and are.

I believe we may be at a watershed in the evolution of a new tough-minded breed of leaders who not only won't shy away from love, but will perceive the intrinsic power in it. What are the implications for our jobs? Our families? Our team? Our lives? The story of Big Ed may help to provide some insights.

I arrived in a city to present a seminar on tough-minded management to a group from many different organizations. I was met by a group of people who took me to dinner to brief me on the people I would talk to the next day.

The obvious leader of the group was Big Ed, a large, burly man with a deep, rumbling voice. At dinner he informed me that he was a trouble-shooter for a huge international organization. His job was to go into certain

Figure 15.2. Action plan for expective living.

Major goal _____   Why? _____

Key result area _____   Why? _____

Action Step	Resource Requirements (skills, money, training, relationships)	Specific Tasks	Target Dates	
			Begin	Complete

Figure 15.3. Weekly planning control sheet.

Specific Task	Completed?	Not Completed?	Alternative Action (if not completed)

divisions or subsidiaries to terminate the employment of the executive in charge.

"Joe," he said, "I'm really looking forward to tomorrow because all of the guys need to listen to a tough guy like you. They're gonna find out that my style is the right one." He grinned and winked.

I smiled. I knew the next day was going to be different from what he was anticipating.

The next day he sat impassively all through the seminar and left at the end without saying anything to me.

Three years later I returned to that city to present another management seminar to approximately the same group. Big Ed was there. At about ten o'clock he suddenly stood up and asked loudly, "Joe, can I say something to these people?"

I grinned and said, "Sure. When anybody is as big as you are, Ed, he can say anything he wants."

Big Ed went on to say: "All of you guys know me and some of you know what's happened to me. I want to share it, however, with all of you. Joe, I think you'll appreciate it by the time I've finished.

"When I heard you suggest that each of us, in order to become really tough-minded, needed to learn to tell those closest to us that we really loved them, I thought it was a bunch of sentimental garbage. I wondered what in the world that had to do with being tough. You had said toughness is like leather, and hardness is like granite, that the tough mind is open, resilient, disciplined, and tenacious. But I couldn't see what love had to do with it.

"That night as I sat across the living room from my wife, your words were still bugging me. What kind of courage would it take to tell my wife I loved her? Couldn't anybody do it? You had also said this should be in the daylight and not in the bedroom. I found myself clearing my throat and starting and then stopping. My wife looked up and asked me what I had said and I answered, 'Oh, nothing.' Then, suddenly, I got up, walked across the room, nervously pushed her newspaper aside and said, 'Alice, I love you.' For a minute she looked startled. Then tears came to her eyes and she said softly, 'Ed, I love you, too, but this is the first time in twenty-five years you've said it like that.'

"We talked a while about how love, if there's enough of it, can dissolve all kinds of tensions, and suddenly I decided on the spur of the moment to call my oldest son in New York. We had never really communicated well. When I got him on the phone, I blurted out, 'Son, you're liable to think I'm drunk, but I'm not. I just thought I'd call you up and tell you I love you.'

"There was a pause at his end and then I heard him say quietly, 'Dad, I guess I've known that, but it's sure good to hear. I want you to know I

love you, too.' We had a good chat and then I called my younger son in San Francisco. We had been closer. I told him the same thing and this, too, led to a real fine talk like we'd never really had.

"As I lay in bed that night thinking, I realized that all the things you'd talked about that day—real management nuts and bolts—took on extra meaning, and I could get a handle on how to really apply them, if I really understood and practiced tough-minded love.

"I began to read books on the subject. Sure enough, Joe, a lot of great people had a lot to say and I began to realize the enormous practicality of applied love in my life, both at home and at work.

"As some of you guys here know, I really changed the way I worked with people. I began to listen more and to really hear. I learned what it was like to try to get to know people's strengths, rather than dwelling on their weaknesses. I began to discover the real pleasure of helping people build their confidence. Maybe the most important thing of all was that I really began to understand that an excellent way to show love and respect for people was to expect them to use their strengths to meet objectives we'd worked out together.

"Joe, this is my way of saying thanks. Incidentally, talk about practical! I'm now executive vice-president of the company and they call me a pivotal leader. OK, you guys, now listen."

CHAPTER **16**

THE G FORCES OF THE FUTURE

We must dare to confront our possibilities.

A look into the future can be daunting and discouraging, or it can be pulse-quickening, exciting, and challenging. The tough-minded leader will welcome the future with open arms and an open mind, with anticipation and joy.

Let's pull together a few of our recent achievements, look at them, and attempt to see precisely where we are. We are a few million creatures on a piece of planetary material drifting—with purpose, we hope—through a vast and uncharted macrocosm. To what end?

Management practitioners and pundits have been concerned with the following management basics for a number of years.

1. The management process: Plan, organize, execute, coordinate, and control

2. Involvement and commitment
3. Management by objectives (call it what you will)
4. Results measurement
5. Accountability
6. Reduction of individual and intergroup conflict
7. Communication and motivation
8. Performance standards
9. Organization planning and design
10. Maximization of profit

We've focused on these, and they have paid off—at least partially. On the stage of international commerce, we've lost a step. We must dramatically accelerate the development of leadership and technological innovations if we are to remain competitive in world markets.

Significant changes must occur in the value systems of leaders, changes that bring a greatly heightened interest in the positive potential of other people. The final goal—here and now, and perhaps forever—is to achieve abundance of the human spirit. From this spirit flows all innovation, all creativity, and all else that is renewing. From this spirit comes the motivating power—the G forces of the future. The end of tunnel vision may be in sight.

HEADLAMPS FOR TOMORROW'S MINES

As new leaders seek to mine the riches of the human spirit, they must strive always to free themselves from the negative pull of the G forces of the past. Here are some ideas for people who want to remove the straitjacket of obsolescence. These statements range from criticism and recommendations to challenges. They are all intended to shed light on a murky future.

☐ Are you ready for the age of cybernetics, synergy, and high touch / high tech? (If you have to look up the meaning of two or more of these words, you may be pretty obsolete already!)

☐ Did you know that the only usable equipment all of us take to work each day is our *minds?*

☐ Would your team continue to follow you if you had no rank, title, or vested authority? Would the quality of your mind expressed through example be sufficient?

☐ Do you agree that the leading society in the world in the year 2000 will be the one that has won the race for *inner* space, the space between the ears?

☐ Did you know that America still produces approximately 40 percent of the world's wealth with 6 percent of the world's population? If we subtract all the nonbusiness people from that 6 percent we would have about 1 percent left. If we subtract all nonmanagement people from that 1 percent we would have only a small fraction of 1 percent of the world's population represented by American business leadership. This tiny fraction is the group that has been most responsible for the great increase in the world's level of material abundance, still so woefully short of its potential.

☐ What if this same group—these managers and potential leaders of American businesses—were to become informed and committed to abundance of the human spirit? Faith is seeking adventure in new dreams, new territories, new methods and techniques—moving boldly into uncharted ways.

☐ Foundations are allocating large sums for studies into the causes of addictions and illnesses. Suppose greater amounts were spent to study the causes of compassion and confidence? Of human optimization? Of growth and renewal?

☐ Suppose that business were to go all out to sponsor studies on the following negative and positive G forces?

G Forces of the Past	G Forces of the Future
Mental myopia	Mental vision
Fear	Courage
Despair	Hope
Mental illness	Mental health
Sick businesses	Healthy businesses
Economic failure	Economic success
Greed	Service
Dishonesty	Integrity
Fatigue	Energy
Dullness	Brightness
Cynicism	Positiveness
Hate	Love
Insignificance	Significance
Doubt	Faith
Lethargy and mediocrity	Vitality and high energy

There are, of course, many more, but do you see what I'm calling for? *Mental toughness.* People whose mental equipment is flabby will usually choose the easiest and most expedient course in their jobs, in their relations with family, in their total existence. Expedient thinking is poor equipment for the future.

☐ Did you know consultants find that the most common denominator in the organization that has failed, is mediocre, or is about to fail, is—call it what you will—procrastination, finger-pointing, blame fixing, reacting to symptoms rather than to causes? Whatever the label, this tendency represents the dominance of a set of negative and expedient values. Such behavior is always associated with a static or rigid mind.

☐ The higher in the organization an executive moves, the greater the emphasis on qualitative abilities and results and the less emphasis on quantitative abilities. By the time executives become CEOs, their contribution is almost wholly in terms of *qualitative* individual skills (communication, motivation, and example). But they are still measured by that implacable quantitative measurement we call the statement of profit and loss.

☐ There is still a considerable gap between the lip service given to the importance of developing a comprehensive philosophy of leadership and the actual implementation of such a philosophy. It seems we can communicate it better than we can do it.

☐ How practical is a thoughtfully conceived and skillfully communicated leadership philosophy? One might just as well ask, "How practical is motivation?" Many psychiatrists believe that the principal cause of fatigue in America today is a person's failure to have something bigger and more important than self to live for.

☐ We must recognize that thought is the most productive form of labor. This is easy to say, not easy to put into action. However, management should actively implement policies, procedures, philosophy, processes, and practices based on this premise.

☐ What do you know about what your team members really think? Conduct attitude surveys regularly, and develop a consistent pattern of listening and mentoring sessions. Listen, listen, *listen* to the people who do the work!

☐ Do you yourself have a clear idea of what is needed to improve the value of the mind each team member brings to work each day? The value of your profit posture is usually squarely related to the value of your vision, focus, commitment, energy, products, and services. This must be the locus of future leadership training systems.

☐ Two principal concepts represent within themselves a whole armamentarium of tough-minded values: (1) management by example and (2) high expectations. Both depend on the principle that *we become what we think*. The example you provide is the sum total of you on display. The overriding challenge becomes one of stoking the mind so that you are what you say, and what you say is the product of the best program of individual development you can undertake. Only when we do this ourselves can we truly expect the best from team members. Attempting to change the behavior of others without changing our own is nearly always futile.

☐   We do not enhance the dignity of people when we expect less than the best from them in commitment, talent, and effort. They come to know their strengths, their significance, their relevance when they are required to reach deep into their reservoir of strength, skill, and courage to confront the high expectations to which they have given their commitment. Clear and stretching expectations are, indeed, a gift and a lift. They *pull* people into the future.

☐   In common with everyone else, tough-minded leaders have two principal options as they plug into the future or remain shackled to the past. These offsetting options may be expressed in several ways:

—*Build or destroy.* Managers can target their ideals, values, and practices in terms of *building* or in terms of *destroying.* If they ignore the opportunity to *build* people, products, profit, and so on, they have automatically elected to destroy the potential for growth.

—*Good or bad.* We can assume either that people are fundamentally *bad* and must be coped with, or that people are fundamentally *good* and together will build a better department, a better company, or a better world.

—*For or against.* We can elect to express our abilities in terms of what we are *against* and become futile, fragmented people, or we can elect to function as total human beings because we express our abilities in terms of what we are *for.*

—*Reach or drive.* Stretch (lead) or compress (push).

☐   The great leaders of the future will be *fanatic* about excellence of service.

☐   If you fail to plan, you plan to fail.

SOME THOUGHTS ABOUT THE FUTURE

The year 2000, once a benchmark of science fiction, is now very close. We must do our level best to take off our economic, political, social, psychological, and spiritual blinders. Our methodology must shift from effect to cause, from treatment to prevention, from better military technology to better human minds. Increasingly, the "renegade manager" of today will be recognized as the "renaissance leader" of tomorrow.

Imperatives of the twenty-first century include intense worldwide competition, increasingly global markets, and rapid technological change. But how many of America's future leaders *really* appreciate what it will take to succeed in the coming business environment?

Team Members

Increasingly we will see the dissolution of the typical labor-management contracts, contracts that concentrate on legalese and loophole-itis rather than the basic values and beliefs of individuals. Blue-collar workers in the 1990s will have so much interaction with automated equipment on the job that they will need mental refreshment and challenge off the job (or as planned parts of the day's work). This will be a task for both society as a whole and leadership educators in particular. Centers for continuing education and development will expand exponentially.

We will see much more emphasis on an internal climate based on the belief that people—even a small group of them—who know what they are *for* are always in a better position to achieve uncommon objectives than those who know only what they are *against*. The potential for synergistic action and results is much greater. We must go all out to build the concept and reality of one tightly knit, unified team.

Education for Human Optimization

Dr. J. Bonner Ritchie of Brigham Young University advocates that we dissolve our schools of management and start all over again. He may have something there. It is absolutely vital that our schools of business, particularly myopic MBA programs, undertake the value system described in this book. What about comprehensive courses, even college majors, in positive reinforcement? What about massive educational efforts to study the *causes* of joy, health, achievement, and success rather than the causes of gloom, depression, sickness, and failure? It is predicted that education will have moved sharply in this direction by the year 2000. The equipment and techniques needed to implement such teaching and learning can be better discussed by individual specialists; I am simply calling for a sprint toward the light, not a retreat into darkness. *We must confront our possibilities.* Ross Perot says that when business schools tell him they know of no text suitable for teaching the kind of leadership he calls for, his response is, "Use *Tough-Minded Leadership*—it's all there."

It must cease to be intellectually trendy to engage only in dissent and debunking. Suppose the average executive made a strong attempt to understand and apply the core ideas in Immanuel Kant's *Critique of Pure Reason* to the daily job. This would require real pragmatic intellectualism and could produce a kind of mental toughness that would in turn contribute much to both personal and company objectives. The secret of retaining economic power lies squarely in the demonstrated ability to apply our minds in a wise and positive way in the use and creation of financial resources. In short, the perpetuation of meaningful and viable economic power is utterly dependent on mental power.

The Technological Explosion

The dazzling array of new technological resources for the enrichment of the human condition includes biotechnology, computer software in which quantum leaps are becoming the norm, personal computers, fiberoptics, new materials, robotics, and lasers. Biomedical science, for one example, is examining a wide spectrum of issues, including development of human life, gene therapy to correct inherited defects, new drugs based on the body's own proteins, a better understanding of cancer, and replaceable body parts.

Neuroscience is examining how biochemistry helps to determine our behavior. Using that information, scientists are creating medicines that mimic the brain's chemistry in efforts to control Alzheimer's disease, stroke, and depression. Heart attack fatalities should plummet dramatically as the new clotbusters move into general use. The second major breakthrough is sophisticated new methods of angioplasty and nutritional chelation.

Laser technology is still in its very early phases. The U.S. Department of Defense had spent $1.5 billion on the development of high-energy lasers by the mid-1990s; the Soviet Union had met or exceeded that amount. Exciting new laser advances are expected in many areas. Among them:

☐ *Medicine.* Clogged arteries will be opened with lasers. This can revolutionize the treatment of arteriosclerosis.
☐ *Energy.* Laser-created nuclear fusion may produce energy from seawater.
☐ *Communications.* Combined with fiberoptics, lasers can provide hundreds more television channels. Some scientists believe our grandchildren will be watching lifelike three-dimensional holographic TV and movies, courtesy of lasers.
☐ *Scientific research.* Lasers today drill miniscule holes in living cells so that other genetic matter can be inserted. They will likely play a growing role in genetic engineering.

Entirely new and radically different kinds of lasers will appear. As our knowledge of light and matter grows, lasers will make practical what can barely be done today, and make possible what is not yet dreamed of.

The immense possibilities of the new art and science of computerized parallel processing aided by new breakthroughs in application of superconductivity will make even the term *technological quantum leap* seem like an understatement. But, lest we lose sight of our priorities, let's remember this comment from marketing vice-president Buck Rodgers, after his thirty-five years with IBM:

> *Although I've spent my adult life working in a world of high technology, I fervently believe that it will be* people, *not machines, that save this country from drowning in a sea of mediocrity.*[1]

1. *Getting the Best Out of Yourself and Others* (New York: Harper & Row, 1987).

Figure 16.1. The challenge of the future.

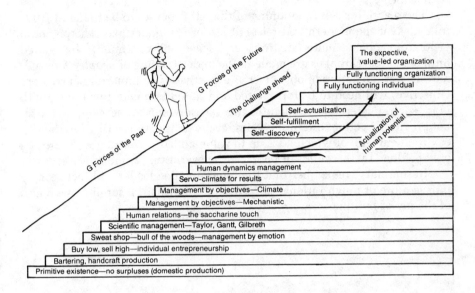

New Galaxies to Conquer?

Will we one day participate in intergalactic and extraterrestrial relationships? If so, will we approach these new worlds with an attitude that we are superior beings who have set out to colonize, establish military bases, and run things in our own way? We don't know. Perhaps we will never know. But while we wait and ponder, we might do well to shift our sights from a dogmatic conquest of outer space to an enlightened conquest of inner space—the latent possibilities implicit in the space between our ears.

A HEYDAY FOR VISIONARY ARCHITECTS

Human progress is slow, sometimes unsteady, but constant. Human possibilities are virtually unlimited if the motive thrust of people is fueled by a positive and relevant system of values. The rewards for the tough-minded person are great. But the hazards are also great, especially if we confuse the search for self-actualization and its emphasis on strengths with the search for self-destruction and its emphasis on weaknesses.

Figure 16.1 illustrates the ascent from a preoccupation with the requirements of stomach and wallet, to an impatient quest for greater significance as a fully functioning person. It shows the evolution of management from static, stratified structures to a synergistic process of leadership. The result will be a fluid, dynamic, and very responsive *whole* made up of fluid, dynamic individuals who possess strong feelings of purpose, relevance, and significance.

The search for full functioning of the self promises to be the most fruitful endeavor the modern and relevant leader can undertake. The potential yield from money, material, time, and space will continue to be limited until new breakthroughs are made in the understanding of *people*. A brand-new look at the nature of objectives as expectives is an important early step. Objectives will need to be formulated and stated in qualitative terms, with more sophisticated use of quantitative measurement. The computer does not provide direction, establish values, or create the stimulating, productive environment—all of which adds up to value-added performance. These can only be done by the minds of people—the everlasting frontier!

In summary, remember that the tough-minded leader will increasingly pursue a life of tough rational purpose and, above all, a surging awareness of the joy of building.

CHAPTER **17**

TOOLING FOR CHANGE

*Change will be the one constant for the rest of your
life. You will never find the ideal management
process or culture.*
LAWRENCE MILLER, PRESIDENT
L. M. MILLER & COMPANY, IN *EXECUTIVE EXCELLENCE*

Attitude is everything. Our attitudes are, of course, a product of our
experience, the information we ingest, the thoughts we think, the words
we use, and the ways other people respond to us. In global terms we must
raise our sights, loosen our biases, and let our minds go forth. Great goals
are never reached until you decide to dare to fail.

We must confront the need for change. Indeed, we must covet and
savor it. We must take decisive steps to put muscle into our dreams.

My colleague Donald Kirkpatrick, professor emeritus from the University of Wisconsin, says the three keys to managing change are 1) empathy,
2) communication, and 3) participation.

THIRTY-FIVE TOUGH-MINDED CONVERSIONS

My colleagues and I have put together a list of thirty-five conversions, changes we believe are essential. They are a distillation of the ideas discussed throughout this book. I recommend it to all dedicated leaders as a working tool kit as you confront the need for change, innovation, and new dimensions of creativity.

From G Forces of the Past	*To G Forces of the Future*
Role orientation	Goal orientation
"Importance"	Significance
Insecurity	Significance
Programs	System
Vague, adequate expectations	Clear, stretching expectations
Defensiveness	Open, war, thoughtful candor
Activity documents and reports	Progress documents and reports
Hunch and guess	Disciplined decisions
Inconsistency	Consistency
Conformity	Individuality
Competing with others	Competing with self
Complexity	Simplicity
Avoidance of problems and needs	Confrontation of problems and needs
Dialogue	Communication
Crises and fire fighting	"Early warning systems"
Office politics	Team synergy
Blurred, expedient morality	Tough, stretching moral climate
Reaction related to symptoms	Action related to causes
Disparate, dissonant actions and procedures	Unity
Compensation based on actions and personal characteristics	Compensation based on positive performance
Fragmentation	Purpose and direction
Getting	Giving
Preoccupation with weaknesses	Building on strengths
Commitment to self only	Commitment to goals and objectives that transcend self
Benign neglect	Caring
Negative listening	Positive listening
*Dis*satisfaction (past-oriented)	*Un*satisfaction (future-oriented)
Gamesmanship	Accountability for results

From G Forces of the Past	*To G Forces of the Future*
Superficial preoccupation with behavioral science jargon	Analysis, evaluation, synthesis, and synergy of tough-minded possibilities
Affirmative-action jargon and dialogue	Evaluating *all* people on the basis of performance
Uncertainty	Self-confidence
Confusion	Viable personal faith beyond self
Physical adequacy	Physical fitness
Grimness	Buoyancy
Passive erosion	Passionate renewal

Conversion No. 1
From: Role orientation
To: Goal orientation

To become enmeshed and trapped by the self-defeating concept of role is counterproductive. The confines are so narrow we hesitate to innovate, take risks, and grow, which means a gradual retreat into the shadows. To leave this orientation behind, it is vital that each person be encouraged, aided, and trained to formulate specific personal goals that are meaningfully related to organizational and work goals. For example, a team member who is role oriented would say: "I am a general assembler." With a goal orientation, this same person would say, "I'm part of the team that delivers the 2000 line of microprocessors on schedule."

Conversion No. 2
From: "Importance"
To: Significance

Policies, procedures, and practices must actually reflect the belief that while importance may be enhanced by compliments and benefits, the true feelings of significance, dignity, worth, and individuality come from an organizationwide focus on strengths and clear, stretching expectations.

Conversion No. 3
From: Insecurity
To: Significance

Feelings of security result in greater productivity and are enhanced when we live and function in an expective environment. Feelings of purpose and direction, which are fundamental human yearnings, provide fuel to function fully, to give feelings of significance.

Conversion No. 4
From: Programs
To: System

One of the major reasons stereotypical management by objectives has generally tended to fall far short of its potential is that diffusion brings about defusion and confusion. To be highly productive, individuals and groups need feelings of consonance, focus, unity, teamwork.

An assortment of projects, procedures, and programs, often random and crisis related, will not meet the pressing needs ahead. System—where the whole consists of smoothly coordinated and synchromeshed components, where real symbiosis and synergy result—is urgently needed. The key building blocks for such a system are the positive G forces described throughout this book.

Conversion No. 5
From: Vague, adequate expectations
To: Clear, stretching expectations

Over many years of consulting, I have been encouraged when I see how individual lives (as well as corporations) begin to change when components of the organization are based on clear and stretching expectations, rather than directives. In reality, the language of the entire organization should change from vague, arbitrary, rigid, sporadic directiveness to clear, evocative, stretching, supple expectiveness.

Conversion No. 6
From: Defensiveness
To: Open, warm, thoughtful candor

It is truly self-defeating to the organization that supplies the paychecks when all communications are approached with excessive caution and defensiveness. Creativity and innovation cannot flourish—or even survive—in such a climate. For real leadership by integrity (which means precisely the same as leadership by strengths) to make a maximum impact on the bottom line, the example must start at the top and be reinforced by clearly communicated expectations based on openness, warmth, candor, and trust. This lets the walls of defensiveness dissolve and sets the stage for real communication to begin.

Conversion No. 7
From: Activity documents and reports
To: Progress documents and reports

In the positive G force climate, three things must be clearly understood:

1. Compensation is directly related to performance.
2. Performance and results are the only criteria for promotions and perquisites.
3. All decisions and assessments are based on performance *progress*.

Therefore all reports should deal primarily with the *progress* being made toward performance commitments.

Conversion No. 8
From: Hunch and guess
To: Disciplined decisions

Since effective, profitable decisions are what the leader is really paid for, there is nothing more vital than that they be made in the most effective way possible. Discipline depends on information that flows out of the consistent application of six ordinary tools: what, where, when, who, how, and why. In addition, major decisions should be processed through:

The A-B-C Principle

Analyze the alternatives.
Balance the benefits.
Calculate the contingencies.

Then *act*.

Conversion No. 9
From: Inconsistency
To: Consistency

If a strategy is to be fully accomplished, it must be planned and executed with consistency and reliability. Inconsistency brings confusion. When you provide consistency of expectations, example, and decisions, people can follow you because energy is focused into productive action. It's like going from the diffused illumination of a light bulb to the concentrated, intensified power of a laser beam.

Conversion No. 10
From: Conformity
To: Individuality

Innovation, creativity, and vitality do not flow from rubber-stamp groups. If the units of an organization are to function in coordinated, synchromeshed fashion, the individuals in them must feel a consistent heightened awareness of:

Present and potential strengths
Involvement in plans and performance standards
Being valued as persons
Being listened to
Clarity of expectations
Compensation tailored to individual results

Conversion No. 11
From: Competing with others
To: Competing with self

When we compete with others, we have a considerable number of built-in copouts. It is so easy to see *something* in others that can lull us into relative complacency and mediocrity. To compete with our own internally generated goals or objectives is to potentially experience our finest hour, to confront our possibilities. When a company or department consistently competes with its own goals, its own self-generated targets, it removes much of the usual grist for internal politicking, finger pointing, gossip, bickering, and other forms of morale-vitiating behavior. It is virtually impossible to even approach optimum productivity when "who gets the credit" is primary. In a department that is truly *led*, team members relish mentioning the accomplishments and pluses of their colleagues.

Conversion No. 12
From: Complexity
To: Simplicity

In our culture, all too often we confuse complexity with difficulty. We are inclined to feel virtuous when we avoid the simple and do the complicated. But in reality, the complicated is easy; it is *tough* to reduce down to simplicity. We must somehow blast the notion that sophistication requires greater intellect and commitment than mastering the basic truths needed to arrive at lean, clean, and clear solutions. The more complex the problem, the greater the need for clear thinking to achieve the simplest (best) solution.

Conversion No. 13
From: Avoidance of problems and needs
To: Confrontation of problems and needs

Nothing erodes confidence and vigor as much as procrastination. This insidious practice can best be rooted out with candid confrontation that blows away the mists of rationalization and stimulates the growth of reality. Procrastination is a prime example of what results from negative G forces. The pull of these insidious factors from the past can produce diffidence, hesitancy, and other forms of anxiety that stultify decisiveness and crisp action.

Conversion No. 14
From: Dialogue
To: Communication

I define *dialogue* as "two or more people engaged in monologues." In contrast, *communication* is "shared meaning, shared understanding." When we truly communicate, superior morale, cooperation, coordination, and control produce superior motivation and productivity. The synergistic synthesis of people, money, materials, equipment, time, and space can truly happen only when *real* communication occurs.

Conversion No. 15
From: Crises and fire fighting
To: "Early warning systems"

The benefits of this conversion are obvious to any thinking manager. Good intentions are not enough in the volatile global arena. The commitment to planning and forward thinking, or tomorrow-mindedness, must flow down from the very top of the organization and should be clearly set forth in the company philosophy. An excellent example of this is item 7 from the leadership pledge of the Marriott Corporation (the complete pledge is found in Chapter 3):

To make sure they always know in advance what I expect [emphasis mine] from them in the way of conduct and performance on the job.

The benefits of such strategic, tactical, and practical planning are enormous. Not only is productivity greater, work is more fun!

Conversion No. 16
From: Office politics
To: Team synergy

Creating the type of climate in which political activity is held to a minimum requires personal leadership of the highest order. For success, positive, tough-minded leaders must:

☐ Recognize that politicking will exist in any organization or group, but that its extent is directly related to leaders' attitudes and that it can be controlled and virtually eradicated by them.

☐ Demonstrate that political activity will not result in benefit to any individual by reacting negatively to political overtures and basing all rewards upon individual contribution to organizational objectives.

☐ Identify political situations quickly and deal with them firmly and openly.

☐ Know when people are making an optimum contribution to the company and when they are not. Key *all* actions to performance.

☐ Have the courage to bring unpleasant personal situations into the open. Be intolerant of hints, innuendoes, or oblique gamesmanship. Require people to say what they think in a candid, straightforward way.

☐ Create the necessary tools and administrative procedures within the organization to ensure that people:

—Know what is expected of them in terms of specific results.

—Know where they stand; when they are doing a good job and when they are not.

—Know why they are working in terms of clearly understood objectives and individual contributions to them.

—See beyond themselves; are as concerned about the company and its welfare as with their own well-being.

—Are rewarded generously for outstanding performance.

The connotation of internal politics is almost always negative. It saps the vitality of a company, creating a climate and spirit in which the full productivity and potential of its people cannot be realized. Truly productive individuals will not become a part of such a climate or remain with such an organization. They know it will drain them of enthusiasm, dedication, ambition, loyalty, and self-satisfaction. Capable individuals want and need to be judged on their worth and contribution. Capable leaders want and need people whose strengths complement theirs.

Conversion No. 17
From: Blurred, expedient morality
To: Tough, stretching moral climate

A searching study of the rise and fall of past civilizations of the world reveals irrefutably that the viability and vitality of each was closely paralleled by the rise and decline of morality. Studies of great corporations that have risen and fallen revealed precisely the same patterns. Good ethics are no longer ancillary to operations. They are more than saccharine slogans. They are crucial. And they are so eminently *practical!* The philosophy of the company must make it absolutely clear that integrity is the beginning and the end of all policies, procedures, practices, processes, programs, and people in the organization. It's good business. I repeat, integrity and strength mean precisely the same thing.

Conversion No. 18
From: Reaction related to symptoms
To: Action related to causes

This is very similar to Conversion No. 11. We tend to *re*act and *re*spond to externally imposed directives. Conversely, we tend to initiate and acti-vate programs, procedures, and practices that stem from our own internally generated expectations. As tough-minded leaders, we truly move forward when we commit ourselves to substituting expectiveness for directiveness.

Conversion No. 19
From: Disparate, dissonant actions and procedures
To: Unity

Modern leaders can learn something from sheepherders. Studies have shown that there is a distinct difference in the quality of the wool of flocks that are driven by the shepherd and flocks that follow the shepherd. Those that were driven were apparently in a constant state of confusion, ran to and fro, and required constant surveillance. They didn't eat well, didn't sleep well, and probably didn't even feel well. Any of this sound familiar? Those that followed a leader could perceive an object—a person—ahead, focus on him with a much higher measure of relaxation and, I venture to say, purpose and direction. They could devote their energies to what sheep do best: eating, grazing, sleeping, and becoming fat, fit, and profitable. Is there a parallel here for you?

Conversion No. 20
From: Compensation based on actions and personal characteristics
To: Compensation based on positive performance

If it was considered desirable to deliberately produce dissension, turn-over, a lowered motivation, creativity, and productivity, one of the most effective ways to do so would be to relate all rewards (money, promotions, recognition, and perquisites) to such things as:

Seniority	Political infighting skills
Education	"Nice-guyisms"
Color, race, religion, sex	Old school ties
Amount of activity generated	Etc., etc.

All elements of the positive G-force climate should be geared to perfor-mance standards. Don't forget, though, that those standards should be devel-oped with appropriate involvement of the team members, and that they should provide and reward stretch. I firmly believe that such a policy can provide even more rapid promotions and greater rewards for high performers.

Conversion No. 21
From: Fragmentation
To: Purpose and direction

Purpose and direction are fundamental to the tough-minded expective company and its tough-minded team. Ideally, *all* people on the payroll understand:

☐ The macro vision, the dream.
☐ The mission, philosophy, goals, and objectives of the company.
☐ The objectives, standards, and action plans of their own organizational units.
☐ The specific authority, responsibility, and, particularly, accountability provisions of and for their own job.
☐ That all rewards and perquisites are based on performance and results.
☐ That doing everything possible to fulfill these multiple expectations will benefit *all*.

Fragmentation, disparateness, and diffusion all add up to negative confusion. Positive ferment, however, can and should be stimulated.

Conversion No. 22
From: Getting
To: Giving

This conversion means everything and it means nothing, depending on our conditioning, experiences, and level of tested insight. It has been my privilege to work with managers who understand the potential practicality of the old axiom "The more you give, the more you get." These leaders have meticulously and tenaciously sought to build this awareness into every person, policy, procedure, practice, and program in their area of responsibility. The person who truly understands this knows that while it does indeed require disciplined effort, the pervasive use of this truth can move their organization far beyond Theories X, Y, and Z.

Conversion No. 23
From: Preoccupation with weakness
To: Building on strengths

The crucial necessity for this conversion is fundamental to everything I've said in this book. Let's hear what a couple of others have to say. According to Robert Heller:

There is only one protection in good times and in bad, and it doesn't lie in technology alone, or even mainly. Play consistently to your strengths and invest consistently in them and you won't need to change your flavor.[1]

And in the words of Peter Drucker:

To build on [a person's] strengths, that is, to enable him to do what he can do, will make him effective. . . . To try to build on his weaknesses will be . . . frustrating and stultifying.[2]

The tough-minded leader knows that building on strengths and positive reinforcement are identical.

Conversion No. 24
From: Commitment to self only
To: Commitment to goals and objectives that transcend self

Throughout America much effort and money are being spent unwisely for "employee motivation," on the basis of the cynical notion that people in general are fundamentally interested in self-serving actions. Research, experience, and deep reflection will reveal to the manager that high levels of motivation are created and built only when members of a team are committed to beliefs that transcend their own wants and needs. History is replete with examples of people who accomplished infinitely more than the sum of their individual efforts could possibly suggest because of stretching—often sacrificial—philosophies.

Every dimension of the great organization of the future will be saturated with commitment to service. We denigrate people's dignity when we assume they do not want to give, build, create, and, yes, to a very real extent, sacrifice. This basic and real need can be met and harnessed for the good of all if we *expect* with consistency, clarity, confidence, and courage.

Tough-minded leaders insist, by precept and example, on moving beyond the idea that people place their creature comforts ahead of giving, serving, and building. In reality, there is a deep human need to grow, change, give, and build. But people need leadership to effectively do so.

Conversion No. 25
From: Benign neglect
To: Caring

Many business organizations stultify the possibilities of their people with paternalism and directiveness. Real compassion requires involvement, lis-

1. *The Supermarketers* (New York: E. P. Dutton, 1987).
2. *The Effective Executive* (New York: Harper & Row, Publishers, Inc., 1966).

tening, building on strengths, clear and stretching expectations. As you study and overhaul your philosophy, policies, practices, and programs, use this tough-minded maxim as a template:

I will not be my brother's keeper unless he cannot keep himself. Rather, I want to be my brother's brother and help him keep himself.

Conversion No. 26
From: Negative listening
To: Positive listening

It is difficult to overemphasize the importance of this conversion. The success of all the instruments in this book depends on it. Possibly nothing can make people feel more ignored, hostile, diffident, or resistant than listening without hearing. Positive or active listening requires listening with mind, heart, and soul—really *hearing*.

Conversion No. 27
From: *Dis*satisfaction (past-oriented)
To: *Un*satisfaction (future-oriented)

*Dis*satisfaction may be defined as "reflecting or being hung up on the failures, insufficiencies, or inadequacies of the past." It is, in effect, parking beside yesterday's failures and using such failures to justify avoiding the challenges of today and tomorrow.

*Un*satisfaction may be defined as "a healthy, restless commitment to discovering and accomplishing that which is better: a better lifestyle, a better policy, procedure, program, or practice." *Un*satisfaction is indeed the stuff of higher motivation and productivity. Satiation is not a happy state for long, but rather a discrete point on life's continuum, a launching site for further achievement.

Conversion No. 28
From: Gamesmanship
To: Accountability for results

The productive and synergistic team needs gamesmanship and one-upsmanship like a hole in the head. The perennial politicians within the organization play a major role in eroding morale, motivation, energy, and positive peace of mind. They are also really tedious people to spend time with. Tedious? Yes! What is more boring and emotionally draining than slyness, innuendo, and sophomoric angles. *Accountability for results* helps ensure the elimination of these factors. Accountability also provides much healthy stimuli in the form of:

Purpose and direction
System and order
Accomplishment criteria
Rewards and reinforcement
Growth of responsible behavior

Conversion No. 29
From: Superficial preoccupation with behavorial science jargon
To: Analysis, evaluation, synthesis, and synergy of tough-minded possibilities

What a challenge to treat this subject without lapsing into the very psychobabble I wish to steer you away from! For example:

"Let us interface."
"I know where you're coming from."
"I hear you saying . . ."
"That's where it's *at.*"
"Here's a warm fuzzy for you."
"Let me 'bottom line' you."
"Let me 'parameterize' the situation."
"Let's consider the infrastructure implication."
"Don't invade my space."

I repeat, we not only become what we think, we become what we *say.* Research has clearly indicated the productive and stimulating power of crisp, emotive, evocative, precise language. When the leader begins to master the art of lean, clean, and meaningful words, followership grows, and this is what leadership is all about.

Conversion No. 30
From: Affirmative-action jargon and dialogue
To: Evaluating *all* people on the basis of performance

This again relates to the need for all levels of our society, including government, business, unions, and all our institutions, to understand the implication of:

I will not keep my brother unless he cannot keep himself. Rather, I want to be my brother's brother and help him keep himself.

When all the Ps in the organization reflect this performance-based emphasis, real dignity and worth are enhanced.

Conversion No. 31
From: Uncertainty
To: Self-confidence

High productivity and profitablity will always elude the uncertain organization that operates with diffidence, defensiveness, procrastination, and diffusion of effort. Philosophy, mission, goals, objectives, action plans, performance standards, building on strengths, compensation based on performance, and all the positive G forces in this book build the self-confidence necessary for profitability and high productivity.

Conversion No. 32
From: Confusion
To: Viable personal faith beyond self

An organization is only as effective as the individuals in it. True motivation, vigor, and, yes, *joy* cannot flourish in a barren soul and mind that exists primarily for personal gain. The prevalence of this wrongheaded notion has contributed much to the lag in productivity and morale we see today. It is basic to the human being to give, to build, to contribute, to believe, and to expect. Therein lies hope, and hope is the universal nourishment of all human beings.

Conversion No. 33
From: Physical adequacy
To: Physical fitness

It is encouraging to note the recent dramatic emphasis on fitness and wellness in business. When days grow long, fatigue can set in. It is only tough-minded common sense to suppose that people will function better and make better decisions when they are fit. I predict, in fact, that "whole person well-being" will receive more attention, money, and effort than any other area in our society in the coming years.

Conversion No. 34
From: Grimness
To: Buoyancy

Somehow the notion has proliferated that grim managers are more practical or tough-minded, that humor is somehow impractical or unworthy of "important" people. Nothing could be more wrong! Would *you* like to work with or follow a grim person with upside-down mouth and extinguished eyes? Tough-minded leaders who are committed to expective rather than directive management, leaders rather than pushers, stretchers rather than compressors, have no time to waste on downbeat, grim, counterproductive practices. Rather, they say in effect, "Follow me and we'll get a lot done and have a lot of fun." You can't do much of one without the other.

Humor and liveliness dissolve grimness, and create the happy chemistry that enriches our lives. Victor Borge says laughter is the shortest distance between two people. Ain't it the truth?

Conversion No. 35
From: Passive erosion
To: Passionate renewal

Real in-depth commitment to passionate renewal in every dimension of your life—and thus in your team members—requires that since no one can live in neutral, you resolve to use every thought, word, and action to *enhance* people rather than diminish them. This is no idle and idyllic challenge. It does, however, require discipline, courage, and love—all *renewing* ingredients. In the next chapter I cover this conversion in detail.

The whole point of this chapter is that if you want to change organizational habits, change the *people*. If you want to change people, make sure that the right nutrients are provided for their *minds*.

CHAPTER **18**

THE POWER OF
PASSIONATE LEADERSHIP

By using their ambitions, talents and capacity, these
leaders have identified true calling, as it were, and
fulfilled their own genius, their visions of excellence
through the application of passion, energy and
focus.
—WARREN BENNIS AND BURT NANUS IN *LEADERS*

My greatest concern up to this point has been *operational* values, traits, and functions of tough-minded leadership. In this final chapter you are invited to examine sixteen elements of a *personal* pattern of growth. Since people must feel that they are excellent before doing excellent work, I invite you to address the sixteen challenges that follow.

THE CYBERNETIC CIRCLE OF
EXPECTIVE GROWTH

The sixteen elements shown on the cybernetic circle of expective growth, Figure 18.1, are presented to add human depth and dimension to the preceding chapters, to aid in building a personal growth path that fuels the growth of the organization. Please ponder them deeply and thoughtfully.

While the spiritual component is related to Judeo-Christian values, it is not intended to exclude other faiths. Although it may seem I have put a disproportionate emphasis on personal growth, the last fifteen years should have taught us that team productivity is impossible without steady and meaningful enhancement of the individual. A team is, by definition, the sum of its individual strengths. Thirty years ago American leaders by and large scoffed at "spiritual values" as crucial dynamics in management. The Japanese have amply demonstrated that we exclude them at our peril.

Since this is a passionate book—about hopeful leading and living—I ask you to take a long, thoughtful look at the cybernetic circle of expective growth. It is at once both an introduction and a summing up, my attempt to "put it all together" in a dynamic configuration of both procedural mechanics and human dynamics. Please join me in exploring the potential of these sixteen elements in the challenging, turbulent, and delightful decades ahead.

Challenge No. 1: Self-Knowledge

The logic and power of the maxim "know thyself" is as old as civilized thought. Today, unfortunately, even though many attempt to know themselves, few succeed, because of a fundamentally flawed education in how to do it. The only reality of a person is his or her strengths. Until this is recognized and built into business, school, government, church, synagogue, home, and workplace standards, we will continue as a community of nations to stay plateaued in our quest toward the far reaches of human possibilities.

We cannot understand a weakness, because a weakness is only an absence, a fault, a zero, a vacuum, a nothing. We can understand and acquire only *strengths*. Once this is fully perceived and understood, once we realize that the only tools, the only building material, the only fuel we possess are our present and potential strengths, we can begin to focus intently on:

What *is* rather than what *isn't*.
What *can* rather than what *can't*.
What *will* rather than what *won't*.
What *does* rather than what *doesn't*.
What *has* rather than what *hasn't*.

Figure 18.1. The cybernetic circle of expective growth.

1. Know what you can and will expect from you.
2. Let yourself perceive all your possibilities.
3. Determine specific components of your dream.
4. Decide on what, where, when, who, how, and why of what you want to be and do.
5. Determine how well the goals can and must be realized.
6. Schedule, prioritize, develop your "life calendar."
7. Apply your mind and skills diligently.
8. Believe in you, in others, and in your own higher power. Believe others are right unless proved wrong.
9. Believe in your experiences.
10. Love is the central source of energy that makes it all happen.
11. The highest form of mental and spiritual health.
12. Let life *in*. Seek, quest, appreciate, enjoy.
13. Dissolve your emotional defenses.
14. Savor the flavor of each passing "now."
15. A sure guarantee of growth, change, and fulfillment.
16. Perhaps this is the finest way to *express* all the other portions of the circle.

Please begin an all-out quest for greater awareness and use of all your current and potential strengths. This is truly the new frontier. The kind of leader you are tomorrow begins in your mind today.

Challenge No. 2: Your Dream

Knowing yourself stimulates and encourages dreams. It is important to let ourselves dream freely and soaringly, or we will not know how to use our mental, physical, and spiritual muscles with any degree of purpose, discipline, and system.

One of the several goals of this book is to provide you with insights, concepts, principles, and techniques for putting muscle into your dreams. But how do we go about defining a dream? What are some of the ingredients of a possible dream?

Our perception of how we should behave in order to believe and become is best served by a dream, a transcendent vision of expectancy. To help put some meaningful sequence into the process, please study Figure 18.2, the continuum of actualization: the possible dream. To aid in this study, ask yourself these seven questions:

1. What would you ideally most like to be?
2. What would you ideally most like to do? (It is important that human *being* should precede human *doing*.)
3. What kind of experiences help you feel more *complete?* (This is symbiosis.)
4. What kind of relationships are most helpful in making you feel multiplied, compounded, increased? (This is synergy.)
5. In what kind of situations do you most want and tend to share yourself?
6. In what kind of circumstances can you most vulnerably let others *in* and let you *out?*
7. What kind of happenings best help you feel a sense of exceeding yourself?

The tough stuff of possible dreams must be fashioned and crafted out of reality. And reality starts with asking, listening, and hearing. The formula looks like this:

Asking,	+	Perceiving,	Guided	Expectations,	=	The
listening,		believing,	and	strengths		Possible
and		and	fueled by	discovery, and		Dream
hearing		becoming		an action plan		

What you imagine is what will transpire. What you believe is what you will achieve.

Figure 18.2. Continuum of actualization: The possible dream.

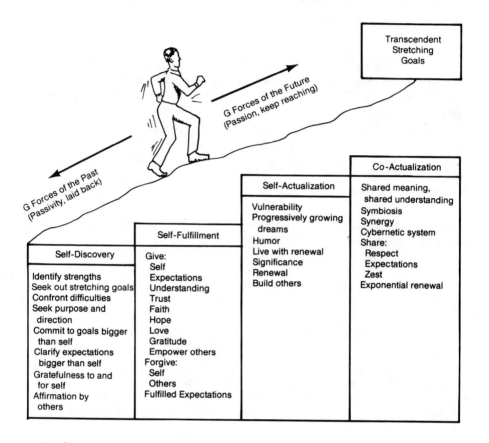

Challenge No. 3: Goals

"Set goals" may be the most frequently chanted dictum of all success experts. The problem is, however, that all too few people know how to go about it.

The entire cybernetic circle (Figure 18.1) has been carefully crafted to provide these steps. Meaningful, stimulating goals must be preceded and nourished by a dream. This gives goals a *being* flavor rather than a self-defeating focus on activities or *doing*. Having a dream also means that goals will be focused on aspirations beyond your immediate knowledge and skill level, thus providing stretch. Consider these areas for goal setting:

Economic, social, political, spiritual
Physical, mental, emotional
Personal, occupational

Goals should be achievable and attainable in order to satisfy clearly charted expectives. It is important, however, that your overall dream provide a continuous need to improve and grow.

My own dream has evolved from years of challenge, joy, difficulties, failures, and triumphs. You will note that it is stated in such a way that it cannot ever be *fully* accomplished: "I will make the lives of others richer by the richness of my own."

I must point out that goal setting doesn't consist *only* of the great and the noble. I think of R.G., an intellectually gifted and highly educated man. When he was promoted to a new position in his company, he talked much about programs, products, and practices to "help the needy in the third—and fourth—worlds." There was no question about the importance of this altruistic goal. However, he reflected so much on these noble purposes that he neglected the need for effective short-range projects like cost control, budget development, and skills training for his staff. He failed to meet his commitments to his employer and was eventually asked to leave the corporation.

Challenge No. 4: Action Plan

Over the years I have heard so many people say, "I want to be . . ." or "I want to do . . ."—and that's about all that happens. *Wanting*, after all, doesn't really accomplish anything. The important thing is to decide to make a *decision*. Only then can we move from good intent into a plan of action that yields results.

In the action plan for expective living shown in Figure 15.2 we begin an orderly process of moving from a dream-inspired goal to specific action steps for achievement. For instance, your key result area here might well be a restatement of your goal. If your objective is to make your life contributing, caring, and rich, your major goal might be to obtain a certain type of job or position, and your key result area might be to gain additional skills, certification, or education.

Number the action steps sequentially and list them in descending vertical order in the "Action Step" column. Carefully think through each step across the page horizontally to the right, and be sure to enter all the components of the complete plan.

One of the major benefits of this process is the disciplined thinking, with accompanying clarity of purpose, that flows out of it. Please don't just glance at this format and conclude it's a fine thing for someone else to do. Think through and complete your own private plan right now.

The CEOs of many small entrepreneurial organizations, in particular, have found this to be a useful point of departure into more sophisticated strategic plans. *Action* is at the core of all achievement.

Challenge No. 5: Standards

As your action plan actually begins to happen, it is crucial that you have some objective criteria, some standards, to guide you so that you know at all times just how you are doing. Standards should be specific, measurable, practical, attainable; they should have a targeted attainment date and state an end result.

Challenge No. 6: Timetable

Note that this step is built right into your standards. Committing yourself to a growth-producing timetable can be very healthy, because you are charting and carrying out self-generated expectives rather than simply responding to directives laid on you by someone else.

Challenge No. 7: Work and Discipline

The common (and commonly misunderstood) phrase "Perception is reality" is useful here in connection with two overworked and underunderstood words: *work* and *discipline*. The way we feel about these two concepts is a direct product of how we perceive their meaning.

Does *work* mean "keeping a stiff upper lip" and making an intrepid pledge to work *hard?* Does *discipline* mean "facing up" to a difficult task? And does any of that sound inviting, energizing, stimulating? Does the thought free you up, make your heart sing? I doubt it.

Remember, we become what we think and we become what we say. It is crucial, then, that we examine the real meaning of *work* and *discipline* in terms of their potential for growth, joy, and fulfillment.

The most successful people are often thought of as "hard" workers, but this is not true at all. The results they have achieved are indeed enormous, but this is not because of rigid commitment or obsessive approach to work. They enjoy work itself. All the great achievers see work as a privilege, an opportunity, a gift.

Discipline is defined as "training which builds, molds and strengthens." This is why it cannot be separated from a zestful concept of work and precisely why it has little relationship to the rigid, morose ideas described earlier. Discipline and its expression, work, can prevail only if nourished by a transcendent goal and by a viable faith in yourself and those around you. Thus your *perception* of work and discipline is your personal reality.

Challenge No. 8: Faith

Faith is an integral part of the kind of value system that enables us to deliver a full payload of happiness, productivity, and actualization.

The interrelationship of faith to the other fundamental needs can be shown in this formula:

Faith + Hope + Love + Gratitude = Significance

Faith is incomplete without hope, love, and gratitude. Love is incomplete without faith and hope. Hope is incomplete without faith and love. Above all, faith without passion is like soda water without the sparkle. Without these renewing feelings of faith, hope, love, and gratitude, our behavior on the job, in the home, and in the community can be marred by insecurity, defensiveness, cynicism, and other feelings that corrode our possibilities.

The sheer practicality of faith on a deep and pervasive level is enormous. Faith and belief, after all, mean the same. And there is practically no limit to what you and I can do if our belief in ourselves, our fellow person, and our own perception of a higher power are strong and constant. In short, faith and success as a total person, a significant person, are totally synonymous.

Challenge No. 9: Hope

I believe hope is the universal nourishment of the human being, and expectations are steps on the pathway of hope. When we get out of bed in the morning, without hope there would be no reason to do anything at all. With ample hope we bring the dream, goals, action plan, timetable, and standards into functional operation.

Challenge No. 10: Love

Socrates, that old master of expective, tough-minded discourse, said it like this: "Human nature will not easily find a helper better than love."

Perhaps the greatest single breakthrough in the enrichment of the human condition will be the widespread realization that love, fueled and completed by faith and hope and synergized by gratitude, is the most practical thing in the world. We are now in the Age of the Mind and all we do that is practical is a product of the mind. The finest nutrient for the mind is love.

Challenge No. 11: Gratitude

Do you have an "attitude of gratitude"? Or do you have "hardening of the attitudes"? You can't have a full measure of both. They cannot coexist. Hardening of the attitudes may very likely be the most insidious and pervasive disease of humankind since the beginning of civilization. Such rigidity has been the root cause of socially and psychologically disintegrating behavior, manifested in a broad spectrum of illnesses, war, crime, and the trillions of petty thoughts and actions that have stultified people and taken the rich bloom from life's possibilities.

I'm not talking about gratitude as an occasional action. I'm talking about a continuous, ongoing process of being or experiencing. At the very least, the "act" of gratitude requires that we summon up an awareness of positives, of good realities, sensed as well as seen. As we gain skill in being and staying aware of these good feelings and experiences, the finest kind of mental nourishment can evolve.

The converse, of course, is true. When our minds are not fed a diet of gratitude, they become breeding places for the darker side of ourselves.

Please examine the following exercise thoughtfully and complete each portion. In each area, replace the negative feeling with a positive. For each one, actually write down something you feel grateful for. I realize this is not easy. It requires most of us to reverse the conditioning of a lifetime. If you care enough to find the "possibility fragments" in each of these situations, real growth can begin.

Negative Feeling	*Positives Perceived*
Alienation from loved ones	_____
Despair	_____
Valuelessness	_____
Boredom	_____
Meaninglessness	_____
Hopelessness, defeat	_____
Dryness, staleness	_____

Gratitude is the essence that can multiply the power of faith, hope, and love. Try it. You'll like it!

Challenge No. 12: Wonder

The sense of wonder is developed through a positive outlook on life. It is a full-time, lifelong quest that persists in seeking out the wonder, the beauty-*enhancing* qualities of people, events, and things.

Perhaps this definition of *wonder* may be useful to you: "To sense, to reach, to hunger and thirst for further assurance of the possibilities in all things. This is the enhancement of a sense of wonder."

Can you think of anything more calculated to retain the emotional resilience and mental elasticity of youth and creativity than a sense of wonder? Out of this vital quality flow many very practical things: greater creativity, innovation, methods improvement, job performance, customer service, unity of family and fellow team members.

Challenge No. 13: Vulnerability

We cannot truly love anyone—ourselves or others—unless we let ourselves be vulnerable. We can sometimes be emotionally hurt in the process, but if we never let ourselves be open to another person—family member, colleague, or friend—we cannot grow as a human being. When we let ourselves be open with others, we can discover in them good qualities we never suspected. As a result, we grow stronger and are able to bounce back from the times when we are rebuffed or hurt by someone. We become more tough-minded in our vulnerability!

I have often used the phrase "Vulnerability is invincible" and I mean precisely that. If you find that hard to believe, give me just one example of significant growth or gain that was not preceded by some testing, trying, tough circumstance.

A major breakthrough becomes possible when we equate emotional vulnerability with courage and strength. What happens to a physical muscle when it encounters *no* stress or resistance? What happens to a mental muscle when it encounters *no* stress or resistance? Do you begin to see the self-destructiveness of a lifestyle rooted in defensiveness, safety, and *invulnerability*?

Can a marathon runner develop toughness and stamina without going through many long, aching hours of effort? Can any man or woman, boy or girl, develop social skills, confidence, poise, and grace without vulnerably engaging in a wide assortment of social activities? Can the timid become courageous in *any* endeavor if they live behind a safe wall of nonconfrontation? Can your team develop unity, synergy, and esprit de corps without undertaking some tough and stretching objectives—and *winning?*

Challenge No. 14: Truth and Beauty

Since we become what we think and say, the nutrients to enrich and toughen our minds are crucial. No matter how skillfully we develop and chart our process of planning and goal setting, we can achieve and sustain the necessary momentum only by thoughts that flow out of truth and beauty. Since the search for truth and beauty has fueled more breakthroughs in technology and human understanding than anything else in history, and since thoughts are the quintessential tools of the future, the tough-minded leader feeds and develops the capacity to think in all logical and feasible ways.

Challenge No. 15: Caring, Sharing, and Forgiving

These are some of the most profound keys to success in life as a whole. To care, share, and forgive is to live at life's cutting edge. As we care, we reach out beyond ourselves. Caring suffuses all superior leadership and full functioning. If we do not care much about others, we will ultimately not care much about ourselves. When we care, we become vulnerable. When we do not care, we become *invulnerable* and *die* a little inside.

To share is to express caring tangibly. It is a further expression of vulnerability, wonder, faith, hope, love, and gratitude. It is the here-and-now, hands-on practical way we help enrich the human condition. Remember, too, that an excellent and appropriate *expectation* is one of the finest things we can share.

Forgiveness is a requisite for happiness and peace of mind, for a liberated and energizing approach to life. The all-too-rare ability to forgive is best developed as part of an overall lifestyle. A lifestyle based on being *for-getting* sets up a collision course with rigidity. Actually, we never truly forget; we simply tuck the "forgotten" feelings into our subconscious. They are still there. In truth, we must remember in order to forgive. As we then develop a lifestyle that is based on *for-giving* we become capable of *forgiving*.

Challenge No. 16: Asking

The importance and power of *asking*, of clear expectations, has been neglected in the literature of effective living and leading. It is the one act that fuses and focuses all the rest.

Most people are unaware that a question is almost always a stronger and more effective approach than a declarative, directive, or commanding statement. Thoughtful, clear, firm, and tough expectives get better results, and allow the other person to retain self-respect and dignity. They are "open sesame's," the initiators of real productive actions. In the future, *telling* will be accurately perceived as obsolete, and asking will be understood as a real power instrument.

The power and importance of asking is beautifully illustrated by the following:

Ask and it will be given you.
Seek and you will find.
Knock and it will open unto you.

It can be tough and zestful—and isn't that what it's all about?

LEAD WITH PASSION

In his fine book, *Unlimited Power* (1986), Anthony Robbins says that there are seven basic character traits of leaders who consistently produce positive results:

1. Passion
2. Belief
3. Energy
4. Strategy
5. Clear values
6. Bonding power
7. Mastery of communication

Of passion, he says:

> *It's passion that causes Pete Rose to dive head first into second base. It's passion that causes people to stay up late and get up early. It's passion that people want in their relationships. Passon gives life power and juice and meaning. There is no greatness without a passion to be great, whether it's the aspiration of an athlete or an artist, a scientist, a parent, or a businessman.*[1]

Passion is indeed powerful stuff and must be used by the pivotal leader in a disciplined, focused, and mentally tough way. The real leader of tomorrow is, above all, a thinker who acts with passion.

TOMORROW, AND TOMORROW,
THE G FORCES BECKON

The greatest companies in the world, those that continue to provide opportunities to build financial, mental, social, and spiritual wealth, were almost invariably launched and fueled by a dream, a macro vision. Out of that dream evolved the "P" pyramids of reality and the goals, objectives, action plans, timetables, and accountabilities of the real world. Progress toward those dreams can often seem faltering and far from perfect, because all of us are pretty imperfect.

Our great and wonderful opportunity, however, is to chart a course of the *possible* dream and dare to keep our sight and senses on it. There may be setbacks and failures, but we will almost certainly have a higher level of accomplishment and actualization than if we have no dream at all.

The sheer practicality of asking and expecting yourself and others to

---

1. (New York: Simon & Schuster).

work harder and smarter in a cause greater than self has been tested through the centuries.

Will you dare to dream? Will you etch out your personal vision?
Will you dare to articulate high hopes?
Will you dare to put muscle into those dreams?
Will you constantly pursue positive possibilities?
Will you expect the best?
Will you dare to become all you can be?

Will you do it?

Remember, tomorrow will not fail you *unless you choose* to throw it away.

It is my sincere hope that a decade from now, thoughtful review and assessment of American leadership will clearly reveal that:

☐ The corporate cultures and megatrends of the 1980s reflected these dares and made the necessary investment of time, money, mind, spirit, and perspiration.
☐ We at last perceived the intrinsic pragmatism, the practicality of suffusing the total culture with a commitment to the enrichment of the human condition.

APPENDICES

The lessons for the future are clear: vision, innovation, renewal, quality, commitment, energy, discipline, and personal leadership can build a great and exciting tomorrow.

The following appendices are included to enhance that message and to provide further insight into what a tough-minded approach entails:

Appendix A: Situational Assessment Guide—From Macro to Micro
Appendix B: The Tough-Minded Leader—Five Positive G Forces
Appendix C: Putting It All Together—The Positive G-Force Climate

APPENDIX A:
Situational Assessment Guide—
From Macro to Micro

The purpose of this assessment guide is to aid the tough-minded leader in building a future-oriented organization that can move into the business vanguard and ride the turbulent waves of tomorrow.

These questions have been tested in hundreds of organizations. There are two parts to the assessment guide, which starts on page 191:

1. G-Forces Analysis (a macro focus)
2. Are You Harnessing Technology for Optimum Information Reporting? (a micro focus)

This appendix was carefully designed for a wide diversity of readers. I have attempted to err on the side of abundance and have sought to provide some aids for a wide assortment of situations and challenges. The macro treatment offered in the general management/leadership analysis was structured to ensure broad and versatile application. The micro focus on the data processing division was designed in the belief that since this function is newer and more complex than most, it requires more specificity and focus.

G-FORCES ANALYSIS

	Yes	No	N/A

POLICIES

1. Are policies clearly defined and written out in a manual? ☐ ☐ ☐
2. Do they accurately reflect the philosophy and grand design of the company? ☐ ☐ ☐

PLANNING

1. Have company objectives and standards been thoroughly defined for
   a. Productivity? ☐ ☐ ☐
   b. Innovation? ☐ ☐ ☐
   c. Physical and financial resources? ☐ ☐ ☐
   d. Marketing? ☐ ☐ ☐
   e. Manager performance and development? ☐ ☐ ☐
   f. Worker performance and attitude? ☐ ☐ ☐
   g. Public responsibility? ☐ ☐ ☐
   h. Profitability? ☐ ☐ ☐
2. Have personnel evaluation performance techniques (PERT) or critical path methods (CPM) been used to good advantage? ☐ ☐ ☐
3. Are the following steps being taken with a view to profit maximization?
   a. Study of all unusual expenditures and all changes and additions in product, policy, methods, systems, and equipment from the perspective of the long-term as well as the short-term effect on the company. ☐ ☐ ☐
   b. Continuous, organized effort to improve quality and reduce costs as well. (It is necessary for such effort to be *redoubled* when the company is most prosperous and its operations are most profitable.) ☐ ☐ ☐
   c. Continuous development of all products and services, and of inspection standards, to accelerate improvements. ☐ ☐ ☐
   d. Continuous simplification and improvement of existing philosophies, policies, methods, and systems. ☐ ☐ ☐

	Yes	No	N/A

e. Installation of fundamentally new systems, methods, and mechanizations wherever needed. □ □ □

f. Continuous fundamental research on all phases of the company's products and related problems. □ □ □

g. Development of new products and methods of merchandising and distribution, as indicated by market requirements and overall profit value to the company. □ □ □

h. Market investigation of the acceptability or non-acceptability of the company's products and methods of merchandising and distribution. □ □ □

i. Routine, scheduled visits to other plants in both related and unrelated industries to examine and evaluate their policies, equipment, methods, and systems with a view to adaptation and application to the company. □ □ □

j. Encouragement for executives and other team members to take an active part in trade and civic organizations. □ □ □

k. Provision of adequate capital for current and future plans. □ □ □

4. Are business game and simulation techniques used? □ □ □
How?_____

OPERATIONS

.1. *Procurement.*
Are all materials purchased by competitive bid in accordance with specifications, in quantities requisitioned by production control (if applicable)? □ □ □

2. *Production control and scheduling.*
Is production completely planned and scheduled in accordance with marketing requirements and manufacturing facilities? □ □ □

3. *Plant engineering.*
Is plant location determined by studies of material and labor supply and market locations? □ □ □
Are plant facilities arranged in accordance with production methods and processes? □ □ □

4. *Tool engineering.*
Are tools developed, designed, and tested to yield the lowest feasible manufacturing cost for each product? □ □ □

	Yes	No	N/A
5. *Manufacturing.*			
Are high-quality, low-cost products the rule?	☐	☐	☐
How is this determined?_____			
Are modern methods of plant layout used?	☐	☐	☐
Which ones?_____			
What is the proportion of direct labor to indirect labor?_____			
How much production is presently scrap?_____			
Is full computer-integrated manufacturing targeted?	☐	☐	☐
How measured?_____			
Are schedules met?	☐	☐	☐
How far in advance are they planned?_____			
Are methods improvements attempted?	☐	☐	☐
Check method used:			
a. Flow process charts	☐	☐	☐
b. Layout and flow diagrams	☐	☐	☐
c. Work distribution analysis	☐	☐	☐
d. Time and motion studies	☐	☐	☐
e. Other_____	☐	☐	☐
6. *Quality control.*			
Is quality control a separate function?	☐	☐	☐
Is quality control used as an aid to sales and manufacturing?	☐	☐	☐
How?_____			
Are deviations from quality specifications permitted during periods of peak delivery requirements?	☐	☐	☐
Has quality control improved the design of products and processes?	☐	☐	☐
How?_____			
Have possible applications of statistical quality control been studied?	☐	☐	☐
7. *Value analysis assurance.*			
Are any or all of the foregoing functions being analyzed 100% in terms of *value contribution?*	☐	☐	☐
8. *Product/service analysis.*			
Have the specific product lines or services been determined which will yield the greatest return for the resources expended?	☐	☐	☐
Do you gather and chart the following sales data?	☐	☐	☐
a. Sales by product line (last five years)	☐	☐	☐
b. Gross profit by product line (last five years)	☐	☐	☐

	Yes	No	N/A
c. Share of market by product line (last five years)	☐	☐	☐
d. Total market by product line	☐	☐	☐

Do you gather and chart the following distribution data?

	Yes	No	N/A
a. Sales and gross profit by channel of distribution (last five years)	☐	☐	☐
b. Sales and gross profit by customer (Pareto analysis should show that about 20% of customers account for 80% of sales).	☐	☐	☐
Do you analyze the allocation of the company's resources with respect to its sources of greatest profit?	☐	☐	☐
Do you identify the transactions that generate costs and measure their variability by product line?	☐	☐	☐

For example:

	Yes	No	N/A
a. Number of sales orders processed	☐	☐	☐
b. Number of factory orders issued	☐	☐	☐
c. Number of invoices sent out	☐	☐	☐

GENERAL CONTROL

	Yes	No	N/A
1. Is there a system of standard costs?	☐	☐	☐
2. Does it reflect all variances between standard and actual costs?	☐	☐	☐
3. Are variances from standard performance supplied currently to management?	☐	☐	☐
4. Are there unnecessary accounting records?	☐	☐	☐
Has this been analyzed recently?	☐	☐	☐
5. Are all control records integrated?	☐	☐	☐
6. Are estimates for product pricing based on standard costs?	☐	☐	☐
7. Is provision made for management to keep currently informed on the effect of sales mixture and product selling prices on total company profits?	☐	☐	☐
8. Are breakeven graphics used by each major department to reflect the effect of additional volume cost and profit?	☐	☐	☐
9. Are there budgetary controls?	☐	☐	☐
10. Is there an adequate system of reports on the performance of all departments?	☐	☐	☐
11. Is there a system of commitments?	☐	☐	☐

12. Are operative research administrative procedures, records, forms, and reports designed to produce re-

	Yes	No	N/A
quired information at lowest cost? Give examples:			
_____	☐	☐	☐
13. Are accounting data supplied promptly, in the form best adapted to use by management?	☐	☐	☐
Is modern accounting equipment used?	☐	☐	☐
14. Are perpetual inventories and stock control maintained?	☐	☐	☐
15. For what length of time are forecasts prepared?	☐	☐	☐
16. Are controls too few?	☐	☐	☐
Or are they too numerous?	☐	☐	☐
17. Are controls *understood?*	☐	☐	☐
18. Are controls dynamic instruments for profit maximization?	☐	☐	☐
19. Are key decisions made by accessing computerized strengths banks?	☐	☐	☐

HUMAN RELATIONS

	Yes	No	N/A
1. What are people doing *to* each other?_____			
2. What are people doing *for* each other?_____			
3. Do members believe in the purpose of the organization?	☐	☐	☐
4. Do they believe in their leadership?	☐	☐	☐
5. Do they believe in each other?	☐	☐	☐
6. Do they communicate and participate with each other effectively?	☐	☐	☐
7. Do they feel free to express their views?	☐	☐	☐
8. Do they believe in the company?	☐	☐	☐
9. Is the executive group cohesive?	☐	☐	☐
10. Who helps whom?_____			
11. Who goes to whom?_____			
12. Which executives appear to be only partially accepted?			
_____			
Why?_____			
13. What kinds of personal adjustment problems are there?_____			
14. Are "bosses" too busy to see their people?	☐	☐	☐
15. Are "subordinates" afraid of their "bosses"?	☐	☐	☐
16. What kinds of friction are there?_____			
Why?_____			

ORGANIZATION STRUCTURE

	Yes	No	N/A
1. Does it work effectively?	☐	☐	☐
By what yardsticks?_____			
2. Does the informal organization work against the formal organization?	☐	☐	☐
How?_____			
3. What kind of informal subgroups or cliques have been formed?_____			
4. What marked splits are there between various levels of management or between management and employees?_____			
5. What is the social hierarchy?_____			
What are the status symbols?_____			
6. Do people understand and accept the organization structure, line of command, and delegation of authority and responsibility?	☐	☐	☐
7. Do individuals have an opportunity to use their initiative and demonstrate their ability to grow?	☐	☐	☐
8. How accurately do formal job descriptions, organization charts, or performance standards reflect the jobs of executives as they themselves describe them?	☐	☐	☐
9. Is the organization structure simple and flexible?	☐	☐	☐
Or is it inflexible and complex?	☐	☐	☐
10. Are subordinate units relatively self-sufficient?	☐	☐	☐
11. Have levels of supervision been kept to a minimum?	☐	☐	☐
12. Has the number of specialized activities been kept to a minimum?	☐	☐	☐
13. Are all executive positions, including first-line positions, truly management positions?	☐	☐	☐
14. In moving up, have executives taken important parts of their old duties with them?	☐	☐	☐
15. Are waste effort and waste motion common?	☐	☐	☐
Where?_____			
16. Can key decisions be made at relatively low levels?	☐	☐	☐
17. Are strengths being deployed logically at all levels?	☐	☐	☐

MANAGEMENT EFFECTIVENESS

	Yes	No	N/A
1. Is there any evidence of in-depth planning?	☐	☐	☐
What kind?_____			
2. Do executives direct, delegate, and coordinate effectively?	☐	☐	☐

	Yes	No	N/A
3. Do they initiate effective action and work with others cooperatively?	☐	☐	☐
4. Are they committed to the development of people?	☐	☐	☐
5. Do people know where they stand with their supervisors?	☐	☐	☐
6. Do executives tend to procrastinate over critical decisions?	☐	☐	☐

Why?_____

What is the decision-making process?_____

	Yes	No	N/A
7. Is the organization drifting? Are its energies fragmented?	☐	☐	☐
8. Is the leadership process autocratic?	☐	☐	☐
9. Are any executives concerned about working relationships among their subordinates?	☐	☐	☐

Why?_____

	Yes	No	N/A
10. Is there any evidence that executives are concerned about self-development?	☐	☐	☐

What evidence?_____

	Yes	No	N/A
11. How do subordinate executives view superior executives?	☐	☐	☐
12. Do all team members feel empowered to innovate?	☐	☐	☐

EFFICIENCY OF WORK METHODS

	Yes	No	N/A
1. Are executives methods conscious and economy minded?	☐	☐	☐
2. Are standard operating procedures disorganized?	☐	☐	☐
Is their purpose understood?	☐	☐	☐
3. Are written instructions meticulous and thorough?	☐	☐	☐
4. Do written instructions appear to conform to present methods?	☐	☐	☐
5. Have jobs been simplified to the point where people can no longer have any real interest in their work?	☐	☐	☐

6. What areas appear to be most suited for methods improvement?_____

	Yes	No	N/A
7. Can work layout be improved?	☐	☐	☐
8. Do people show any evidence of being conscious of or interested in improving their work?	☐	☐	☐
9. Is PERT, CPM, or value analysis being used?	☐	☐	☐
10. Is the relationship of procedures to objectives understood?	☐	☐	☐

QUALITY OF PERSONNEL PRACTICES

	Yes	No	N/A

1. How are individual executives and employees selected?_____
   What criteria are used?_____
2. Has the selection procedure been formalized in writing? ☐ ☐ ☐
3. Are tests used? ☐ ☐ ☐
   Are these current and appropriate? ☐ ☐ ☐
4. What provision is there for training and development? ☐ ☐ ☐
5. What is the basis for promotion?_____
6. Do pay rates correspond to levels of work? ☐ ☐ ☐
7. Have salary ranges been developed on the basis of result rather than activity factors? ☐ ☐ ☐
8. Are all employees kept informed about company matters? ☐ ☐ ☐
   Do they feel they are an integral part of the company? ☐ ☐ ☐
9. How do people feel about their jobs?_____
10. Are they, generally speaking, in the right jobs? ☐ ☐ ☐
11. Have supervisors and executives been selected for their leadership ability? ☐ ☐ ☐
12. Are personnel policies continually reviewed for pertinence and relevancy? ☐ ☐ ☐
13. Are they incorporated in manuals and distributed? ☐ ☐ ☐
14. Is the incompetent person kept on the job? ☐ ☐ ☐
    Or have steps been taken to eliminate him or her? ☐ ☐ ☐
15. Is there a program of job evaluation? ☐ ☐ ☐
    Is it achievement or activity oriented?_____
16. How are staff people used?_____
17. Are staff and line functions discernibly different? ☐ ☐ ☐
18. Do morale and discipline seem satisfactory? ☐ ☐ ☐
    Is this reflected in the company's safety records? ☐ ☐ ☐

UNION-MANAGEMENT RELATIONS

1. What is the attitude toward the contract?_____
2. What period of time is covered by the contract?____
3. How are relationships with the union representatives?
   _____
4. Are union rules being followed in spirit as well as word? ☐ ☐ ☐
   Are the rules understood? ☐ ☐ ☐

	Yes	No	N/A

5. Is there any evidence of insincere practices designed to undermine the union's position? ☐ ☐ ☐
6. Do employees view the union as their protector? ☐ ☐ ☐
7. Is there cooperation with, rather than appeasement of, the union? ☐ ☐ ☐
8. Is there codetermination? ☐ ☐ ☐

BOARD OF DIRECTORS

1. Do current directors have a grasp of company problems? ☐ ☐ ☐
2. Are they a sound blend of broad-gauge and specialized people? ☐ ☐ ☐
3. What are their backgrounds?_____
4. Are they identified strongly with the company? ☐ ☐ ☐
5. How are directors compensated?_____
6. Is emphasis on:
   a. Policy determination?____% ☐ ☐ ☐
   b. Future planning?____% ☐ ☐ ☐
   c. Current operational problems?____% ☐ ☐ ☐
   d. External conditions?____% ☐ ☐ ☐
   e. Internal conditions?____% ☐ ☐ ☐
   f. Profit planning?____% ☐ ☐ ☐
   g. Innovation and change?____% ☐ ☐ ☐
   h. Internationalization?____% ☐ ☐ ☐
7. Is there:
   a. An audit committee? ☐ ☐ ☐
   b. A compensation committee? ☐ ☐ ☐
   c. A nominating committee? ☐ ☐ ☐
   d. An executive committee? ☐ ☐ ☐
   e. An innovation committee? ☐ ☐ ☐

GENERAL ADMINISTRATION

1. Are all instructions channeled through a precisely defined organizational structure? ☐ ☐ ☐
   Or are they given directly to those selected to achieve them? ☐ ☐ ☐
2. Are committees named only for specific purposes and kept small? ☐ ☐ ☐
   Do they meet promptly at regular intervals with additional meetings only as required? ☐ ☐ ☐
3. Does each major department head hold staff meetings at least once in three weeks? ☐ ☐ ☐

	Yes	No	N/A

4. Are all decisions involving more than one person or more than one division or department the result of consultation with all necessary persons? □ □ □

5. Are adequate notes kept of all group discussions and decisions? □ □ □
   Are they issued to all appropriate participants? □ □ □

6. Does every executive give full consideration to the ideas of superiors, peers, and subordinates? □ □ □

7. Are the ideas of all employees freely exchanged for the overall benefit of the company? □ □ □
   Is there a suggestion or profit improvement plan? □ □ □

8. Do all executives have, at all times, a clear understanding and a complete listing of the company's general and specific objectives and policies, as well as the objectives and policies that apply to their own division or department? □ □ □

9. Do all executives prepare a list of their duties and responsibilities for their superior and require similar lists from those reporting to them? □ □ □
   Do both they and their subordinates know the results required of them? □ □ □

10. Are simple written instructions given where feasible? □ □ □

11. Have all supervisors learned to organize and schedule their work? □ □ □

12. Do all executives put the company's welfare above their own immediate personal interests? □ □ □
    How do they manifest this?_____

13. Do all executives carefully choose and thoroughly train a competent understudy? □ □ □

14. Do all executives delegate authority to their team, place responsibility upon them, and define their accountability for results wherever possible? □ □ □

15. Do all executives deliberately arrange to provide themselves with ample time for thought, study, and profitable planning for the future? □ □ □

16. Do all executives encourage their team to develop initiative and use their own judgment to the greatest practical degree? □ □ □

17. Are team members so competent that it is unnecessary, and hence undesirable, for their superiors to check anything but end results? □ □ □

	Yes	No	N/A
18. Are individuals' accomplishments recognized and appreciated?	☐	☐	☐
19. Are new positions filled and promotions made from within wherever possible?	☐	☐	☐
20. Are promotions made in accordance with ability, loyalty, cooperation, and total contribution to the company?	☐	☐	☐
21. Is there continuous analysis by division and department heads to eliminate unnecessary functions, jobs, procedures, paperwork, reports, and duplication of effort?	☐	☐	☐
22. Are all established procedures carefully audited by division and department heads at stated intervals to prevent deterioration or lapse?	☐	☐	☐
Are they periodically reexamined for possible improvement?	☐	☐	☐
23. Are the company's policies, aims, and plans explained to all executives and supervisors?	☐	☐	☐
24. Are there oversensitive prima donnas, "big wheels," agitators, parasites?	☐	☐	☐

How are they manifested?_____

_____

	Yes	No	N/A
25. Are there incentives for every employee? (This includes department heads and all subexecutives, as well as technical and clerical personnel.)	☐	☐	☐
26. Do sound methods of performance measurement exist?	☐	☐	☐
Is the performance of every employee appraised periodically? Is there individual counseling with a view to merit increases (according to schedules adopted by the company) or upgrading whenever appropriate?	☐	☐	☐
27. Do executives and other employees speak often and with pride of the company's products and methods, where praise is merited, to increase the company's reputation?	☐	☐	☐
28. Is the company a stimulating and electrifying place to work?	☐	☐	☐
29. Is a sincere and pervasive emphasis on service, quality, and innovation discernible in all the Ps in the "P" pyramid?	☐	☐	☐
30. Is a computerized strengths bank in operation?	☐	☐	☐

ARE YOU HARNESSING TECHNOLOGY FOR OPTIMUM INFORMATION REPORTING?

COMPUTER NETWORK CENTER CONTROLS

General Considerations	Yes	No	N/A
1. Is the computer network center under the leadership of a tough-minded leader?	☐	☐	☐
2. Are the computer network center's long-range plans focused on meeting the company's objective?	☐	☐	☐
3. Do you have strategic computer plans for handling the company's future growth?	☐	☐	☐
4. Do you employ current hardware and software in its computer operations?	☐	☐	☐
5. Do you exert the necessary leadership to get the desired level of data processing services?	☐	☐	☐
6. Do you motivate personnel to do an effective job in providing the desired level of data processing services?	☐	☐	☐
7. Do you exercise the necessary control over operations so that fraud, theft, and inaccuracies of data processing methods and procedures can be detected?	☐	☐	☐
8. Do you use the appropriate security measures to minimize fraud, theft, and inaccuracies?	☐	☐	☐

Organizational Considerations			
1. Is the computer network center operating as a separate unit without direct integration into company operations?	☐	☐	☐
2. Is the computer network center centrally located for best use?	☐	☐	☐
3. Are the following personnel groups, located within the computer department, organizationally and physically separate from one another:			
a. Computer operators?	☐	☐	☐
b. System analysis and programmers?	☐	☐	☐
c. Computer supervisory personnel, and auditors?	☐	☐	☐
Are all computer programmers and operators frequently transferred to different equipment and programs?	☐	☐	☐

Procedures and Methods	Yes	No	N/A
1. Are there established written procedures for all data processing activities outside the computer center?	☐	☐	☐
2. Is there standardization for system flowcharts and program flowcharts?	☐	☐	☐
3. Are programming techniques standardized within and monitored by the computer center?	☐	☐	☐
4. Are there established procedures for software and program testing?	☐	☐	☐
5. Have all standardized procedures been compiled in appropriate manuals?	☐	☐	☐
6. Is the computer manual current?	☐	☐	☐
7. Are there established procedures for making program and networking changes?	☐	☐	☐
8. Are all program changes immediately documented, including the reason for the change?	☐	☐	☐
9. Is computer-integrated manufacturing a myth or a reality?	☐	☐	☐

INPUT CONTROLS

General Considerations

	Yes	No	N/A
1. Does electronic data processing (EDP) management require that input controls be made an integral part of its information system?	☐	☐	☐
2. Are newer input controls instituted by EDP management to reflect changing conditions of input methods and procedures, such as from a batch processing mode to an interactive mode?	☐	☐	☐
3. Does EDP management require that input start with the first input processing methods and procedures?	☐	☐	☐
4. Are input controls reviewed periodically by an independent third party (consultants or auditors) to make sure that they serve the purpose for which they were intended?	☐	☐	☐

Verification Methods

	Yes	No	N/A
1. Are all important data fields verified to ensure accuracy of input information?	☐	☐	☐
2. Is the degree of accuracy adequate?	☐	☐	☐

Yes   No   N/A

3. If conversion equipment and data transmission equipment are used to convert or transmit data (input), is adequate verification being performed? ☐ ☐ ☐

Input Control Totals

1. Are all input documents prenumbered and accounted for by an independent count so that all transactions received are processed? ☐ ☐ ☐
2. Is responsibility fixed for errors on input documents so that corrective action can be taken? ☐ ☐ ☐
3. Are input-error corrective methods properly controlled to ensure that actual correction and reentry into the system is accomplished? ☐ ☐ ☐

PROGRAMMED CONTROLS

General Considerations

1. Are programmed controls required by DP management? ☐ ☐ ☐
2. Are programmed controls fully understood and implemented by the programming staff? ☐ ☐ ☐
3. Are programming controls reviewed periodically by an independent third party, i.e., consultants or auditors, to make sure that they service the purpose for which they were intended? ☐ ☐ ☐

Validation Checks and Tests

1. Is sequence checking used to verify the sorted input data? ☐ ☐ ☐
2. Are data fields checked for correct type of data: alpha, numeric, zero, blank, and special characters? ☐ ☐ ☐
3. Do code numbers, such as account number and inventory number, make use of the self-checking digit techniques? ☐ ☐ ☐
4. Are limit or reasonableness tests used where needed? ☐ ☐ ☐
5. Do programs test input data for valid costs, and are printouts or halts provided when invalid codes are detected? ☐ ☐ ☐

	Yes	No	N/A
6. Do programs make use of checkpoints when processing must be restarted after its initial start?	☐	☐	☐
7. Do computer loading routines include tests that verify the successful loading of a computer program?	☐	☐	☐

Computer Control Totals

	Yes	No	N/A
1. Do computer programs provide continuance of input control?	☐	☐	☐
2. Are the following control techniques used in the various computer programs:			
a. Balancing totals?	☐	☐	☐
b. Cross-footing balance checks?	☐	☐	☐
c. Zero balancing?	☐	☐	☐
d. Proof figures?	☐	☐	☐
e. Other?	☐	☐	☐
3. Are the completeness and accuracy of the various files checked during processing?	☐	☐	☐
4. Are changes in program rate tables and other data initiated in writing and under the control of authorized personnel?	☐	☐	☐
5. Are program changes retained for audit?	☐	☐	☐
6. Is there an online procedure for detecting and skipping bad portions of magnetic tape?	☐	☐	☐
7. Are all halts, excluding end-of-job, recorded and retained for audit?	☐	☐	☐

Error Routines

	Yes	No	N/A
1. Is there an adequate program procedure for identifying, correcting, and reprocessing errors?	☐	☐	☐
2. Are all instructions to computer operators set forth in writing for effective processing control as well as handling of error conditions?	☐	☐	☐
3. Are console operators cautioned not to accept oral instructions and not to contact programmers directly when errors are found?	☐	☐	☐

OUTPUT CONTROLS

General Considerations

	Yes	No	N/A
1. Are output controls specified by EDP management?	☐	☐	☐

	Yes	*No*	*N/A*
2. Are newer output controls instituted by EDP management to reflect conditions of output methods and procedures, such as from a batch processing mode to an interactive processing mode?	☐	☐	☐
3. Does EDP management require that output controls be made an integral part of its information systems?	☐	☐	☐

Output Control Totals

1. Can output data be compared with predetermined totals?	☐	☐	☐
2. Are provisions made within the information system to reconstruct files in the event that the current files are damaged or destroyed?	☐	☐	☐
3. Are corresponding transactions being stored in reprocessible form for emergency operations?	☐	☐	☐

Control by Exception

1. Are all exception items immediately and properly investigated?	☐	☐	☐
2. Is corrective action undertaken for all exception items?	☐	☐	☐
3. Is there a periodic verification of master file balances, such as inventory and payroll, to correct erroneous data and check for irregularities?	☐	☐	☐

Control Over Operator Intervention

1. Are procedures in force that prevent access of operators and other unauthorized personnel to programs for perpetuating fraud?	☐	☐	☐
2. Are word processor–consoled printouts controlled and reviewed by designated personnel, such as internal auditors?	☐	☐	☐
3. Is effective control exercised over the operator's adherence to processing procedures?	☐	☐	☐

INTERACTIVE CONTROLS

General Considerations

1. Are interactive controls required by EDP management?	☐	☐	☐
2. Are interactive controls fully understood and implemented by the systems staff?	☐	☐	☐

	Yes	No	N/A
### Online Processing Controls			
1. When input/output terminals are used for data transmission, are the following control techniques used:			
a. Message identification (identifies each message received by the computer)?	☐	☐	☐
b. Message transmission control (assures that all messages transmitted are actually received)?	☐	☐	☐
c. Message accuracy check?	☐	☐	☐
2. Is there adequate control over terminals in case it is necessary to retransmit data?	☐	☐	☐
3. Is access to confidential information properly controlled?	☐	☐	☐
### Diagnostic Controls			
1. Are diagnostic programs, in conjunction with a supervisory program, used to detect and isolate error conditions for proper corrective action?	☐	☐	☐
2. Are there sufficient online programmed controls to handle the following conditions?			
a. Restart the program in question.	☐	☐	☐
b. Reexecute the faulty instruction.	☐	☐	☐
c. Switch control to an error routine.	☐	☐	☐
d. Shut down part of the system.	☐	☐	☐
e. Halt the system.	☐	☐	☐
3. Are checkpoint records developed as processing occurs, to facilitate a restart?	☐	☐	☐
## SECURITY CONTROLS			
### General Considerations			
1. Are security controls required by EDP management?	☐	☐	☐
2. Are security controls fully understood and implemented by the systems staff?	☐	☐	☐
### Specific Considerations			
1. Are master files stored under conditions that provide reasonable protection against damage or destruction?	☐	☐	☐
2. Is there a schedule of all current computer programs that includes an identification number, date, and description?	☐	☐	☐

	Yes	No	N/A
3. Are all computer programs properly documented?	☐	☐	☐
4. Are computer programs and supporting materials maintained in the records library and issued to persons with written authorization?	☐	☐	☐
5. Are adequate daily equipment logs being properly maintained?	☐	☐	☐
6. Are adequate daily equipment logs being reviewed for irregularities?	☐	☐	☐
7. Is entrance to the computer room limited to authorized personnel?	☐	☐	☐
8. Are there procedures for preventing premature reuse of magnetic tapes and disks?	☐	☐	☐
9. Are there adequate controls to prevent premature erasures of data from magnetic tapes and disks?	☐	☐	☐
10. Is there an established policy for retiring magnetic tape reels with excessive read or write errors?	☐	☐	☐
11. Is the computer system serviced by qualified service engineers on a regular basis?	☐	☐	☐
12. Are manufacturers' temperature and humidity requirements maintained?	☐	☐	☐

Finally, are all computer resources subjected to:

	Yes	No	N/A
Constant scrutiny?	☐	☐	☐
Constant change?	☐	☐	☐
Constant improvement?	☐	☐	☐

APPENDIX B:
The Tough-Minded Leader—
Five Positive G Forces

1. A tough-minded leader provides transcendent or macro vision and magnetic lift and pull, like a compass. A tough-minded leader provides purpose and direction.
2. A tough-minded leader provides a crystal-clear focus of all strengths in the organization. Knowing that our strengths are our tools, a tough-minded leader expects and reinforces the *best*.
3. A tough-minded leader is committed to people, service, innovation, and quality. A leader believes this commitment is liberating and enriching to all.
4. A tough-minded leader leads by example that is focused, stretching, and positive. A leader is motive led and value fed.

5. A tough-minded leader ensures that all compensation is related to positive performance and expects total integrity. A leader is guided in all decisions by these two components.

The problem is not the competitor.
The problem, the challenge, is the person in the mirror. And
the *solution* is the person in the mirror.

APPENDIX C:
Putting It All Together—
The Positive G-Force Climate

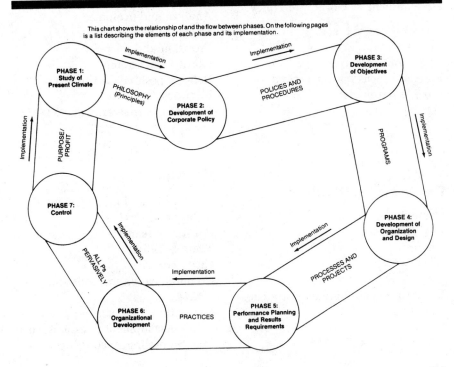

This chart shows the relationship of and the flow between phases. On the following pages is a list describing the elements of each phase and its implementation.

Descriptions of Phases	*Descriptions of Implementation of Phases*

PHASE 1:
Study of Present Climate

Vision/dreams
Quality and service
Strengths assessment
Strengths focus
Spirit
Renewal forces needed
Maturity of current G forces
Survey questionnaire
Diagnostic interviews

PHILOSOPHY (Principles)

Transcendent vision
Mission statement
Macro-goals and focus
Guide principles
Transcendent lift and pull
Expective and positive G forces

PHASE 2:
Development of Corporate Policy

Corporate compass
Lift and pull
Guide and reassure
Fuse and focus motive-action
Provide parameters
Strategic

POLICIES AND PROCEDURES

Analyze and evaluate
Sequence and order
Precision and purpose
Clarity and stretch
Reflects positive Gs throughout
Logistics
Pervasive empowerment

PHASE 3:
Development of Objectives

Strategic planning
Leadership
Service
Quality
Growth
Innovation and human optimization
Profit

PROGRAMS

Leadership and management
Selling and service
Possibility teams
Team building
Customer care
Communication methods and practices
Motivation methods and practices
Other developmental sessions, such as counseling, mentoring

PHASE 4:
Development of Organization and Design

Planning, development, and design
Organization
  Research
  Analysis
  Evaluation
  Synthesis
  Strengths deployment
  Training and implementation

PHASE 5:
Performance Planning and Results Requirements

Performance standards
Performance-based compensation
Accountability
Communication
Tactical and action plans

PHASE 6:
Organizational Development

Coordinate
  Coach and train
  Integrate value system
Execute
  Delegate
  Action plans
  Make policy decisions
  Accountability
Strengths building

PHASE 7:
Control

Management information system
People primacy
Calibrate progress
Optimum computerization
Future focused and user friendly
Lift and pull

PROCESSES AND PROJECTS

Value-added
Definitive position descriptions
Organization schema
Strength-based performance appraisals
Computerized strength banks
New strength deployment tactics
Recruiting
Staffing
Organizational manual

PRACTICES

Strength-based performance appraisals
Reverse all G forces
Reflect reversals in a pervasive manner throughout

ALL Ps PERVASIVELY

Build new positive G forces into all communication, conversations, electronic mail, meeting agendas, memoranda, etc.
All team members in the enterprise must develop pride and unity in and with the company, must feel involvement and commitment to philosophy, goals, and objectives of the business.

PURPOSE/PROFIT

Economic, social, political, and spiritual
Research, teach, and generate all four dimensions of free enterprise.
Constantly seek new ways to better practice positive G-force leadership.

GLOSSARY OF
TOUGH-MINDED TERMS

accountability The "ability to account" for the extent to which a commitment is met.

action plan A sequenced and prioritized chronology of intent, commitment, and tactics: what one is going to get done and some of the key activities involved.

activity Motion toward a clearly targeted result, something one *does*, as contrasted with something one gets *done* (result).

aggressiveness Initiative that is primarily self-serving. Not to be confused with *assertiveness*, which uses one's strengths for purpose of building.

analyze To divide the whole into its component parts (who, what, where, when, how, why) in order to determine the nature, proportion, function, and relationship between the parts.

215

appraisal   To determine the value and possibilities implicit in a person's performance and personality at a particular time.

assertiveness   The vulnerable exposure of strengths. Since strengths are all we possess, and thus all we have to assert, vulnerability permits the full use of these strengths without defensiveness.

builder   The CEO who stands tall is, above all, a builder. Committed to vision, stretch, empowerment, synergy, responsiveness, and flexibility—toughness of mind—a builder ensures that all dimensions of each P in the pyramid are intensely focused on creation, growth, and *building*.

candor   Applied truth. In the tough-minded lexicon, this involves openness, vulnerability, awareness of the needs of others, and a genuine desire to build them.

caring   Consistent manifestation of concern for and affirmation of others. The perception that all people are right until proved wrong and that each person is a bundle of strengths and possibilities.

climate   The temperature of the human environment in which one finds oneself; the "feel," the "chemistry," often more sensed than known.

climate for mistakes   An environment that calls for and reinforces constant experimentation, creativity, innovation, and change. Encourages the practice of "failing forward." Mistakes within reason are *rewarded* rather than penalized.

coach   To help others develop insights and actions to achieve mutually understood goals. This pertains particularly to helping one identify, surface, fuse, and focus one's present and potential strengths.

collaborate   Coordination in action. A blend of strengths to produce positive symbiosis and synergy.

commitment   An internalized, then externalized, concentration of desire and energy focused on various degrees of achievement. An "integrity of intent."

communication   Shared meaning, shared understanding.

compensation   Providing or receiving full value, psychological or financial, for energy expended in accomplishing results.

confront   To address openly, honestly, and vulnerably that which needs to be addressed. The reverse of expedience, obliqueness, deviousness, or avoidance.

consistency   Consonance of unity of thought, word, or deed over a continuum of time, space, or relationships.

consultive decision making   A decision-making process in which the leader involves team members and secures their best input prior to making any major decisions. The tough-minded leader places a premium on asking, listening, and hearing. Thus, when he or she makes a decision and stresses the logical deployment of strengths, team members are expected to meet lean, stretching commitments. Clear-cut accountability is a crucial operational requirement here.

control   An end result of interactive processes involving clarity of expectation and the achievement thereof. Control is not a tool per se. It is a *result* of excellence in applying the other concepts in the tough-minded leadership system.

coordinate   Shared meaning and shared understanding that permit and require the synchronized effort of appropriate people to achieve mutually understood goals.

counsel   See "coach." They are indivisible.

criticize   To evaluate the results of analyses and identify the values or strengths therein. To build on those strengths in seeking to improve the situation, person, or thing.

culture   The pervasive philosophy, central values, beliefs, attitudes, and practices of an organization, and the micro elements that make things happen.

customer-led automated marketing system (CLAMS)   A total operational system fed by imaginatively programmed touch-screen computers to provide constant and comprehensive customer input as a basis for ongoing evaluation and improvement of the entire "P" pyramid.

cybernetic   (From the Greek word, *kybernetes*, meaning "helmsman.") A self-correcting system whose function is perpetuated by a closed loop or servomechanism.

develop   To generate, synthesize, nurture, and ultimately create something better.

dignity   The worth, significance, and uniqueness of a person; an awareness of intrinsic worth. Clear, consistent expectations and a constant search for and focus on strengths affirm this dignity.

directive   Words or actions, felt or implied, that arbitrarily indicate an action or result desired. Tends to suggest "compression and pushing" rather than "evoking and stretching" (as in expective).

discipline   Training and development that builds, molds, and strengthens; lean, clean, focused behavior.

dissatisfaction   A preoccupation with *past* failures; a tendency to dwell on what didn't work. On the contrary, *un*satisfaction is a healthy, hungry desire to change, grow, and move onward and upward.

dream   A deeply felt hope of the possible. Dreams lift and move individuals and organizations to the highest levels of performance.

emotional conflict   A blend of emotions needed to ensure that knowledge or information is transmuted and transmitted into learning. A gestalt of feelings.

empower   To create and foster a relationship in which the other person or persons understand their significance, possibilities, and strengths. People who are empowered have a clear understanding of their authority, responsibility, accountability, and valued role in the team, and they have autonomy that is symbiotic with others.

empathy The imaginative projection of one's consciousness into the consciousness of another. The ability to put yourself in the other person's shoes.

evaluate To identify the relative value of a person, place, thing, or relationship; the values (strengths) revealed by the analysis.

excellence What happens when you give an undertaking your best shot—and know it.

exemplar Leaders whose personas and actions represent the essence of what they say and expect.

expectation A desire, want, or need communicated in the form of a clear request. The ultimate gift, it says to others, "I value and appreciate your possibilities."

expective A more specific statement of expectation; a clear oral or written request. As contrasted with a directive, it is designed to stretch rather than to compress, to *pull* rather than to *push*.

faith Belief in and commitment to causes, quests, and affirmations that transcend self-concern.

feedback Information that clearly indicates the progress and corrective needs of the ongoing project or undertaking.

flexibility and resilience The opposite of *rigidity*. The living and committed responsiveness to possibilities, difficulties, and opportunities.

free enterprise Freedom of individual action to chart and accomplish a full measure of individual achievement—economically, politically, socially, and spiritually; freedom to develop the whole and apply full talents to stretching work assignments.

gestalt A structure in which the response of a person or an organism to a situation is a complete whole rather than simply the sum of the parts or elements; a total configuration of factors.

G forces The figurative pull of gravity. Negative G forces of the past are passive, self-defeating attitudes, and practices that retard and even reverse growth and forward movement. Positive G forces of the future are passionate attitudes and practices that help pull and guide the leader to move toward the future in the most productive, energetic, and positively magnetic way. Like a compass, positive G forces guide and pull.

goal Something one wishes to accomplish. Broader and more timeless than an objective. Expressed as a desired and targeted happening.

go-giver A positive term replacing the cliché "go-getter"; a tough-minded person who knows that one can achieve much more when major energies are directed toward giving encouragement, knowledge, inspiration, and understanding to others rather than seeking self-aggrandizement only.

grace   A special warmth felt and expressed toward all other human beings; an absence of pettiness and self-concern. A living manifestation of the belief that a person should devote major energies to doing something *for* others and not *to* others.

gratitude   Thoughts, feelings, and actions that reflect and transmit appreciation and earned praise.

hard   Rigid, compressed, repressed, depressed, oppressed, brittle, dead, weak. The *reverse* of toughness.

incident file   A document in which key episodes (both positive and negative) are recorded. To be used for developmental coaching and counseling.

individual   In the tough-minded vocabulary, this term means the opposite of a rebel. Rebels live, talk, and work in terms of what they are *against;* individuals live, talk, and work in terms of what they are *for.*

innovation   Newness in action. Ever-searching, ever-changing concepts, methods, research, and application.

integrity   Strength, reality, authenticity, toughness.

intuitive leadership   The demonstrated capacity to take correct actions without necessarily knowing why. Accurate guesses, whether educated or merely sensed. A feel, a sense, a sensation in the gut of what is appropriate. Quick and ready insight.

involvement   Joint and shared use of talents to develop, clarify, and achieve symbiotic relationships and synergistic results.

job description   A listing of key result requirements that constitute or define a job or position.

judge   To form subjective conclusions about another. Judgments project our negative feelings about ourselves into others; they are a projection of weaknesses. The reverse of *evaluate.*

key result areas   Major areas of an individual position or job. They are usually determined so that objectives or standards will be established for all significant responsibilities of the position. Term may also be used to apply to a major emphasis of an enterprise or project.

kinesics   "Body English." The study of body movements, facial expressions, and so on as ways of communicating.

lead   To be in front, figuratively. To lift, guide, expect, empower, communicate, and achieve synergistic results.

leadership   The exercise of a system of expectations—an ever-changing, ever-dynamic gestalt of interacting minds—designed to mobilize and maximize the most effective use of strengths to achieve objectives.

leadership by expectation   Leadership in which a complete and pervasive system of expectations is established throughout the organization and is fueled by the logical deployment of strengths. Leadership by expectation involves the belief that *people* are the alpha and omega of all organizational success. Such a leader practices virtually all the principles and methods in this book.

leadership by renewal   The consistent practice of the principles and methods in this book with primacy given to the belief that *all* team members are more productive and actualized when they are reaching, growing, involved, empowered, and discovering new feelings of individual *significance*. It is a tough-minded axiom that a leader must first *become* this kind of person in order to provide true leadership by renewal.

love   A feeling of brotherhood and good will toward other people. Tough-minded leaders express love via a disciplined commitment to *build* rather than to *destroy*, to *enhance* rather than to *diminish*, all associates and team members through every thought, word, and action. Although it is an ideal, the TML seeks to build this emphasis on enhancement pervasively throughout the organization's "P" pyramid.

loyalty   A quality or action of steadfastly adhering to one's beliefs in a person or thing by every thought, word, or action.

management by objectives   A management style where, ostensibly, all decisions and actions are executed for the purpose of achieving and exceeding clearly defined and agreed-upon objectives.

management process   In the tough-minded management lexicon, this means the following sequence: Research, vision or mission, plan, organize, coordinate, execute, control.

mission   A stretching, guiding, and reinforcing statement of intent and commitment.

motivation   Motive-action; "action to achieve motive." First, *motive* (results, objectives, goals) is developed and then action plans are designed to accomplish them.

negative   Any action that involves retreating from the challenge and discipline required to achieve positive results.

nice guy   One who is affected, self-deprecating, insincere, overly subtle; hence, evasive and untrustworthy. Used in this context to mean a person who chooses the easier alternative and rationalizes this action with "nice" clichés. One who retreats from the requirements of demanding self-discipline.

nurture   To provide insights, expectations, reinforcement, asking, listening, and hearing that *grow* people.

objective   Something one wants to *get done*. A specific statement of quality, quantity, and time values.

open listening   Truly open "hearing" with heart, mind, and soul. A felt and expressed desire to truly understand the other person.

organization "Organ in action." In business, government, and other kinds of endeavor, the collective functioning of a group to achieve mission, goals, and objectives.

organize To blend resources logistically to achieve objectives; to deploy strengths logically.

passion Intense, focused feelings fed in synchromeshed conjunction by the value system described in this book.

passive Yielding, quiescent, nonresponsive, with a low level of reaction. The "bland leading the bland."

performance Discernible and productive actions moving beyond target or intent and actually fulfilling commitment.

performance standards A baseline level of achievement. Commonly defined in the literature as "A standard indicates performance is satisfactory when . . ." Meeting standard performance is the basic requirement for maintaining a position. Extra rewards should be bestowed only when the standard is exceeded.

philosophy A body of truths and firm beliefs. Organizationally, it is the basis for the development of mission, goals, objectives, organization, expective action plans, and controls.

plan An orderly assortment of actions designed to fulfill a mission or accomplish a goal or objective. An objective by itself is not a plan; it is only the basis for one.

positive stress The opposite of negative stress, which causes dissonant disaster and distress; positive stress is healthy, intensely focused energy applied to positive goals.

possibility team A dynamic group of people who blend strengths to discover, recommend, and achieve innovative improvement in all dimensions of the organization.

power Qualities emanating from the leader that exert compasslike pull, both subtle and overt. Such qualities provide both direction and attraction, purpose and pull. Positive, forward-focused influence.

"P" pyramid The pyramidal triangle that presents the following sequence of Ps: philosophy (principles), policies (programs), procedures (processes), practices (projects), and profit (purpose). These Ps represent the complete infrastructure of any organization.

presence A total appearance or impression projected by an individual, which emanates confidence and effectiveness and inspires the confidence of others.

purpose An overriding, lifting, stretching end to be attained.

quality The degree of excellence a thing possesses. Also see **total quality**.

rebel A person who knows, and is primarily motivated by, what he or she is *against*; to know what one is against and be motivated accordingly. See also **individual**.

renewal Innovation and renovation. The process of making fresh, strong, and good; new physical, mental, and spiritual strength.

renewal organization The type of organization in which all the Ps, with emphasis on the people, are geared toward the practice of the contents of this book.

respect Feelings, felt and expressed, that reflect enhanced awareness of the dignity, worth, and individuality of another person.

responsibility Response-ability, or "ability to respond." Responding fully to the pledge of a commitment; responding in a manner consistent with full integrity.

results The final happening. Not to be confused with a *measurement* of a result.

self-actualized Focused, activated, and fueled by the entire value system in this book with particular emphasis on clarity of expectations, building on strengths, and enhancement and empowerment of the team. The self-actualized leader lives and works within the context of a transcendent vision of the possible.

self-confidence The belief that you are significant and good. A growing awareness of one's own strengths and, often, a heightened zest for strong, testing, and confrontive challenges.

self-discipline Commitment of self—in discipleship—to worthwhile courses of action, of programs of development and fitness. Most effective when focused on goals that transcend personal gain.

service The ongoing product of a passionate commitment to fulfill the wants, needs, and possibilities of others.

servo-system A closed-loop cybernetic process that provides for macro-organizational feedback and responsiveness as well as micro-individual feedback and responsiveness. Such macro and micro servo-systems will make possible the kind of responsiveness to customers that must shape the volatile leadership wave of tomorrow.

significance The feeling that a person "counts," is real and is accomplishing good, stretching, and relevant things in life.

social gestalt A dynamic interweaving of individual behavior patterns that produces group accomplishment greater than the sum of its parts.

sophisticated Artificial, highly complicated, refined; maintaining a facade that obscures the basic truths of the situation.

strategy A careful plan or method focused on macro goals. Completed, fulfilled, and sometimes exceeded with the aid of tough-minded tactics—micro-focused action steps.

strengths The true *realities* in all things. Conversely, weaknesses are only what is absent or lacking. Strengths are the *only* building blocks in *anything,* the only resources one can employ in every dimension of life. The meaning of *strength* and *integrity* is the same.

strengths bank   A computerized data base containing the salient strengths of all relevant personnel. This bank is accessed regularly to truly practice the logical deployment of strengths. All major assignments are made and decisions are conditioned by such deployment. Since strengths are indeed the only *reality* in a person, the strengths bank enables an organization to move forward on the basis of total reality. Weaknesses are regarded merely as missing strengths or insufficiently developed strengths.

stress   See **positive stress.**

stretch   A questing, reaching, searching for a better way.

symbiosis   A relationship where living or working together provides and enhances mutual advantage.

synergy   Since all that goes up must ultimately converge, synergy is the magnified impact of a confluence or synthesis of strengths. In shorthand, 2 + 2 = 5 or more. The whole is greater than the sum of the parts.

synthesize   To combine the values and strengths of the individuals discovered during an evaluation.

system   Dynamic reciprocating aggregate of sequenced actions to achieve properly determined objectives.

system of values   A complete and functionally compatible combination of essential truths. Values are the subjective interpretation of the immutable laws of the universe that shape and guide human reactions. The orderly expression and transfer of tough-minded values into practices is the essential process involved in building a climate of productivity.

team   A combination of people, or other productive units, working in dynamic and positive conjunction with each other to produce synergistic results. A group that shares a common toughness of mind.

theory X   A management style described by Douglas McGregor in *The Human Side of Enterprise.* It illustrates the reverse of all that is advocated in this book by stressing the use of organizational rank and directiveness as one's first expedient.

theory Y   Another management style created by Douglas McGregor. It places a premium on caring about people and empowering them to give their best efforts to team accomplishment. It is in general agreement with TML.

theory Z   A management style described in William Ouchi's book *Theory Z,* it is based on thirteen steps practiced by leading Japanese companies. This approach derives from numerous applications of tough-minded management techniques initially introduced to Japanese businesspeople by Konosuke Matsushita, then chairman of the board of Matsushita Industries. He has credited Batten, Batten, Hudson & Swab as the source of these seminal techniques.

tomorrow-mindedness An approach in which all the Ps in the organization are designed and instrumented to anticipate, create, and innovate to meet the requirements of the future. A tomorrow-minded leader is *responsive* rather than *reactive*.

tool A usable resource or combination of resources to *instrument* a desired level of achievement. Something one usually employs directly to get something done.

total quality Integrity of function and composition, from alpha to omega.

tough The integrity of a substance, person, place, thing, or feeling. Characterized by tenacity, resilience, flexibility, durability, and suppleness.

tough-minded Open, resilient, growing, changing, questing, stretching quality of mind. Having an infinite capacity for growth and change. See **tough** and **tough-minded leader**.

tough-minded leader The kind of leader who, much like a compass, provides direction and, figuratively, magnetic pull. The TML "walks in front of the flock" and exemplifies the system of values and practices that this book is all about.

trust The feeling that expectations will be met. The implicit belief in the integrity, or strength, of the potential behavior of another person.

unity Oneness of purpose, focus, communication, and action.

***un*satisfaction** A healthy and hungry desire for new growth, new effectiveness, new levels of achievement. The reverse of *dis*satisfaction.

value The intrinsic worth (or strength) of anything. See **system of values**.

value added A product or service to which has been added features and benefits to *delight* the customer.

value system A dynamic, reciprocating, and reinforcing conjunction of values.

vision A transcendent view of the possible.

visioneering Having vision fed by a synergistic blend of resources tooled for actual achievement. The term we use to describe the tough-minded leader's kit of tools for the future.

vital Bursting with life and positively directed energy.

vulnerable Openness to experiences. Affirmation of belief in the essential goodness and rightness of life. The absence of defensive, petty, or suspicious behavior.

warmth Emotion and caring, flowing toward others, that transmits feelings of affirmation, reassurance, and love. Overt evidence of a desire to build and give to another, reflected in tone of voice, facial expression, and the free expression of positive emotion.

"we" feeling This occurs when one particularly enjoys the practice of giving earned praise to others and when commitment to goals of the organization transcends personal wants, needs, and problems. Reflected in speech by use of "we" in favor of "I." The feeling that one is part of a hard-hitting team that gets results. Ironically, this feeling is possible only when people feel like individuals—with individual purposes, values, and dignity focused on a common goal.

wisdom The ability or gift of transcendent vision. To see the "big picture," to visualize the immediate need or problem in proper perspective. A knowledge of fundamental truths and the ability to use them in a meaningful developmental and positive way, producing a course of action that achieves desired results.

yeast A volatile blend of organic substances that creates synergistic growth. The "good bacteria" are the organizational components treated in this book. The "bad bacteria" are the components of directiveness, expedience, rigidity, and other elements of style that will not meet the requirements of a turbulent tomorrow.

THE NEW LEADER'S BOOKSHELF

Literature on the kind of vanguard leadership I'm advocating is still skimpy, but beginning to grow. Here, as they occurred to me, are a few high quality viands to begin your leadership banquet:

Memos for Management, James L. Hayes (New York: AMACOM, 1983)
   Rich in basic leadership nutrients. Jim Hayes has to be one of the most broadly experienced and insightful people in the business. Good stuff!
Feminine Leadership, Marilyn Loden (New York: Times Books, 1985)
   Marilyn Loden has written a courageous, discerning, and seminal book that breaks new ground. In true tough-minded fashion, this book focuses on the *strengths* of women managers rather than on their weaknesses. It provides stimulating guidance for the woman who seeks not to emulate masculine models, but to build effectively on feminine strengths.
Leaders, Warren Bennis & Burt Nanus (New York: Harper & Row, 1985)

Provides solid insights for all who aspire to make the transition from manager to leader.

Effective Managerial Leadership, James J. Cribbin (New York: AMACOM, 1972)

This venerable text on leadership continues to provide enduring and highly useful food for thought.

Passion for Excellence, A, Tom Peters and Nancy Austin (New York: Random House, 1985)

For some real paprika in the leadership stew, this book by the inimitable Tom Peters is recommended. *A Passion for Excellence* effectively challenges aspiring leaders to reach, discover, and grow.

Leadership, James M. Burns (New York: Harper & Row, 1978)

A recognized classic, this book deals with the *transforming* leader and meshes well with the tough-minded paradigm of reversing the G forces through pivotal leadership.

Corporate Cultures, Terence E. Deal and Allan A. Kennedy (Reading, Mass: Addison-Wesley, 1982)

A valid addition to the classic literature of leadership. A seminal book, it is must reading for all who seek stretching leadership concepts.

Peak Performers, Charles Garfield (New York: Morrow, 1986)

The first-rate research and writing of Charles Garfield has provided some excellent and nostalgic affirmation for me. When Leonard Hudson and I wrote *Dare to Live Passionately* (Englewood Cliffs, N.J.: Parker Publishing, 1966), our statement that the key to a great life was "passionate commitment to a transcendent mission" was figuratively received with yawns. "What does *passion* have to do with management?" we were asked. When Charles Garfield told me of the impact this particular statement had on his life, I was gratified indeed. His role in presenting the efficacy of passion over passivity in leadership is significant and valuable.

Quality Without Tears, Philip B. Crosby (New York: McGraw-Hill, 1984)

This book is helping lead the transition from blaming workers for causing quality problems, to a healthy assessment of the manager or leader as the prime source of needed improvement.

"MAC," Elliott Carlisle (New York: McGraw-Hill, 1983)

This whimsical, humorous, and yet highly practical book is a must for your reading list. A precursor to the *one minute manager* (Kenneth Blanchard) genre, it is so pleasant, one realizes only belatedly the hands-on value of its contents.

The Effective Executive, Peter Drucker (New York: Harper & Row, 1966)

Peter Drucker, the doyen of management writers has, of course, developed a smorgasbord of good stuff. This one is my favorite.

The Making of the Achiever, Allen Cox (New York: Dodd, Mead & Co., 1984)
Makes practically no mention of leadership per se, and yet it is packed with information. Items that mesh particularly well with the philosophy of *Tough-Minded Leadership* have to do with the executive's need and ability to be a giver, to make himself or herself vulnerable, to experiment constantly, to make bold decisions, and to "grab hold" of his or her unique strengths. Cox may be one of the most underrated shapers of thought in America today.

American Spirit: Visions of a New Corporate Culture, Lawrence M. Miller (New York: Morrow, 1984)
Don't miss this! Miller's writings clearly indicate that he "has been there."

The Future 500, Craig R. Hickman and Michael A. Silver (New York: New American Library, 1987)
An important addition to the leadership literature.

A truly excellent leadership publication is *Executive Excellence*, published by The Institute of Principle-Centered Leadership in Provo, Utah, which is headed by Stephen R. Covey, Chairman. Cutting-edge authors regularly present provocative and stretching mind nutrients. I am privileged to be in this group.

A few more fine selections sans specific comment are:

CEO: Corporate Leadership in Action, Harry Levin and Stuart Rosenthal (New York: Basic Books, 1985)

The Will to Manage, Marvin Bower (New York: McGraw-Hill, 1966)

Triad Power: The Coming Shape of Global Competition, Kenichi Ohmae (New York: Free Press, 1985)

Organizational Culture and Leadership, Edgar H. Schein (San Francisco: Jossey-Bass, 1985)

The Management Tactician, Edward C. Schleh (New York: McGraw-Hill, 1974)

The Natural Depth in Man, Wilson VanDusen (New York: Harper & Row, 1972)

The Renewal Factor, Robert H. Waterman, Jr. (New York: Bantam Books, 1987)

Excellence in Leadership, Frank Goble (New York: American Management Association, 1972)

INDEX